Netherlands

Everything You Need to Know

Copyright © 2024 by Noah Gil-Smith.

All rights reserved. No part of this book may be reproduced, distributed, or transmitted in any form or by any means, including photocopying, recording, or other electronic or mechanical methods, without the prior written permission of the publisher, except in the case of brief quotations embodied in critical reviews and certain other noncommercial uses permitted by copyright law. This book was created with the assistance of Artificial Intelligence. The content presented in this book is for entertainment purposes only. It should not be considered as a substitute for professional advice or comprehensive research. Readers are encouraged to independently verify any information and consult relevant experts for specific matters. The author and publisher disclaim any liability or responsibility for any loss, injury, or inconvenience caused or alleged to be caused directly or indirectly by the information presented in this book.

Introduction to the Netherlands 6

A Brief History of the Netherlands 8

The Geographical Landscape of the Lowlands 11

Dutch Colonial Legacy: Influence and Impact 14

The Rise of the Dutch Republic 17

Golden Age: Dutch Trade, Art, and Innovation 20

The Dutch East India Company: A Maritime Empire 23

World Wars and Dutch Resistance 26

Modern Netherlands: A Progressive Society 29

Dutch Monarchy: Tradition and Evolution 31

Dutch Democracy: Institutions and Governance 33

Amsterdam: A City of Canals and Culture 36

Rotterdam: Europe's Largest Port City 39

The Hague: International City of Peace and Justice 41

Utrecht: The Heart of the Netherlands 44

Groningen: University Town and Cultural Hub 46

Dutch Language: History, Structure, and Usage 48

Dutch Cuisine: From Stroopwafels to Stamppot 50

Dutch Wildlife: Exploring the Natural Kingdom 52

Tulips and Windmills: Symbols of Dutch Heritage 54

Cycling Culture: Pedaling Through the Netherlands 57

Dutch Art and Architecture: Rembrandt to Van Gogh 62

Dutch Music: From Classical to Electronic 65

Dutch Literature: From Erasmus to Harry Mulisch 68

Dutch Education System: Excellence and Inclusivity 71

Dutch Healthcare: A Model of Efficiency 74

Dutch Innovation: Driving Global Progress 77

Religious Diversity in the Netherlands 80

Dutch Tolerance: Acceptance and Openness 83

Dutch Sense of Humor: Wit and Sarcasm 86

Dutch Sports: From Football to Ice Skating 88

Dutch Design: Sleek, Functional, Iconic 90

Dutch Technology and Engineering: Leading the Way 92

Dutch Transport: Navigating the Lowlands 94

Dutch Economy: Resilience and Prosperity 97

Dutch Environmental Initiatives: Sustainability in Action 99

Dutch Social Welfare: Ensuring Equality 101

Dutch Immigration: Diversity and Integration 103

Dutch Influence on Global Culture 105

Dutch Language and Dialects 108

Dutch Etiquette and Social Customs 110

Exploring Dutch Countryside: Villages and Landscapes 112

Planning Your Visit: Essential Travel Tips for the Netherlands 114

Epilogue 116

Introduction to the Netherlands

Welcome to the Netherlands, a country steeped in history, culture, and innovation. Situated in Northwestern Europe, bordered by Germany to the east, Belgium to the south, and the North Sea to the northwest, the Netherlands is renowned for its picturesque landscapes, charming windmills, and iconic tulip fields.

The name "Netherlands" translates to "low countries," fitting for a nation characterized by its flat terrain and extensive network of rivers, canals, and polders. Much of the land lies below sea level, a testament to the Dutch ingenuity in land reclamation and water management. In fact, around a third of the country is situated below sea level, protected by an intricate system of dikes, dams, and pumping stations.

The history of the Netherlands is rich and complex, marked by periods of prosperity, conflict, and cultural flourishing. From its origins as a collection of independent territories ruled by various dukes and counts to its emergence as a maritime powerhouse during the Golden Age, the Netherlands has played a significant role on the world stage.

One of the defining moments in Dutch history was the Eighty Years' War, also known as the Dutch War of Independence, which culminated in the establishment of the Dutch Republic in the 17th century. This period saw the Netherlands rise to prominence as a center of trade, commerce, and art, with cities like Amsterdam, Rotterdam, and Utrecht flourishing as hubs of innovation and creativity.

The Dutch Golden Age witnessed the heyday of Dutch painting, with artists such as Rembrandt van Rijn, Johannes Vermeer, and Frans Hals producing masterpieces that continue to captivate audiences around the world. This period also saw the rise of the Dutch East India Company, one of the most powerful and influential trading companies in history.

Despite facing numerous challenges, including foreign invasions, wars, and economic downturns, the Netherlands emerged as a modern, prosperous nation in the 20th century. Today, it is known for its progressive social policies, world-class infrastructure, and thriving economy.

The Netherlands is also celebrated for its cultural diversity and tolerance. With a population that includes people from various ethnic, religious, and cultural backgrounds, Dutch society is characterized by a spirit of openness, acceptance, and inclusivity.

In the pages that follow, we will delve deeper into the many facets of Dutch life and culture, exploring everything from its vibrant cities and stunning countryside to its rich artistic heritage and innovative spirit. So join us on a journey through the Netherlands, where tradition meets modernity, and history intertwines with progress.

A Brief History of the Netherlands

The history of the Netherlands is a tapestry woven with threads of conquest, trade, and cultural exchange. Situated at the crossroads of Europe, this low-lying land has been shaped by the ebb and flow of civilizations for millennia.

The story begins in prehistoric times, with evidence of human habitation dating back to the Paleolithic era. Over the centuries, various Celtic and Germanic tribes settled in the region, establishing a patchwork of tribal territories.

By the first century BCE, the Romans arrived, bringing with them the influence of Roman civilization. The southern part of the Netherlands, known as "Germania Inferior," became part of the Roman Empire, while the north remained largely outside Roman control.

With the decline of the Roman Empire in the 5th century CE, the Netherlands saw the emergence of Frankish and Saxon kingdoms. These early medieval kingdoms laid the foundation for the feudal system that would dominate European society for centuries to come.

In the 9th century, the territory of the Netherlands came under the rule of the Carolingian Empire, founded by Charlemagne. Charlemagne's descendants divided the empire into smaller realms, leading to the formation of the County of Holland and other feudal territories in the region.

By the 12th century, the Netherlands began to take shape as a distinct political entity, with the emergence of powerful feudal lords and the growth of trade and commerce. The rise of medieval towns and cities, such as Amsterdam, Rotterdam, and Utrecht, fueled economic prosperity and cultural exchange.

The 16th century marked a turning point in Dutch history with the onset of the Eighty Years' War, also known as the Dutch War of Independence, against Spanish rule. Led by figures like William of Orange, the Dutch revolted against the oppressive policies of the Spanish Habsburgs, seeking religious freedom and political autonomy.

After decades of conflict, the Netherlands declared independence in 1581, establishing the Dutch Republic as a bastion of republican government and religious tolerance. This period, known as the Dutch Golden Age, witnessed a flowering of Dutch art, science, and commerce, as the Republic emerged as a major player on the world stage.

However, the 17th century also saw the Netherlands embroiled in colonial expansion, with Dutch merchants establishing trading posts and colonies in Asia, Africa, and the Americas. The Dutch East India Company, founded in 1602, became one of the most powerful and influential trading companies in history.

The 18th and 19th centuries brought a series of conflicts and upheavals to the Netherlands, including wars with France and the rise of Napoleonic rule. In 1815, the Netherlands became part of the United Kingdom of the Netherlands, which also included present-day Belgium and Luxembourg.

The 19th century also saw the rise of Dutch nationalism and the struggle for political reform. In 1848, the Netherlands adopted a new constitution, establishing a constitutional monarchy and laying the groundwork for modern parliamentary democracy.

The 20th century brought further challenges to the Netherlands, including two world wars and the struggle for colonial independence. Despite these challenges, the Netherlands emerged as a modern, prosperous nation, known for its commitment to social welfare, environmental sustainability, and international cooperation.

Today, the Netherlands continues to play a prominent role on the world stage, as a beacon of tolerance, innovation, and cultural diversity. From its humble beginnings as a collection of tribal territories to its present-day status as a global leader in trade, technology, and human rights, the Netherlands remains a testament to the enduring spirit of its people.

The Geographical Landscape of the Lowlands

The Netherlands, often referred to as the Lowlands, boasts a unique geographical landscape shaped by centuries of human intervention and natural processes. Situated in Northwestern Europe, the country is known for its flat terrain, extensive network of waterways, and iconic windmills.

Central to the geography of the Netherlands is its system of polders, low-lying tracts of land reclaimed from the sea through a process of dyke-building and drainage. These polders, characterized by their fertile soil and lush pastures, form the backbone of Dutch agriculture and contribute to the country's status as one of the world's leading exporters of agricultural products.

The Dutch landscape is crisscrossed by a network of rivers, including the Rhine, Meuse, and Scheldt, which flow from neighboring countries and empty into the North Sea. These rivers play a crucial role in the country's transportation network, serving as vital arteries for trade and commerce.

In addition to its rivers, the Netherlands is also famous for its extensive system of canals, which thread their way through cities, towns, and countryside alike. These canals, originally constructed for drainage, irrigation, and defense, are now a defining feature of the Dutch landscape, providing opportunities for recreation, transportation, and tourism.

Perhaps the most iconic symbol of the Dutch landscape is the windmill, which has been used for centuries to harness the power of the wind for various purposes, including milling grain, pumping water, and sawing timber. While traditional wooden windmills are still found scattered throughout the countryside, modern wind turbines have also become a common sight, generating renewable energy and helping to mitigate climate change.

Despite its low-lying terrain, the Netherlands has a diverse range of natural habitats, including coastal dunes, wetlands, and forests. These ecosystems provide vital habitats for a wide variety of plant and animal species, including migratory birds, amphibians, and mammals.

The Dutch coastline, stretching for over 500 kilometers along the North Sea, is characterized by sandy beaches, dunes, and barrier islands. These coastal areas are vulnerable to erosion and flooding, prompting the Dutch government to implement innovative coastal management strategies, such as beach nourishment and dune restoration, to protect against the threat of rising sea levels and storm surges.

In recent years, the Netherlands has gained international recognition for its efforts to combat climate change and promote sustainable development. From ambitious renewable energy targets to innovative water management projects, the country is leading the way in finding solutions to the environmental challenges facing the modern world.

In summary, the geographical landscape of the Netherlands is a testament to the ingenuity and resilience of its people, who have learned to thrive in a land shaped by the forces of nature and the hand of humanity. From its fertile polders to its bustling cities, the Lowlands offer a glimpse into a country where tradition and innovation coexist in harmony.

Dutch Colonial Legacy: Influence and Impact

The Dutch colonial legacy is a complex tapestry of conquest, trade, and cultural exchange that left an indelible mark on regions across the globe. From the 17th to the 19th centuries, the Netherlands established a vast overseas empire, encompassing territories in Asia, Africa, and the Americas.

One of the crown jewels of the Dutch colonial empire was the Dutch East Indies, present-day Indonesia, which became a key source of spices, textiles, and other valuable commodities. The Dutch East India Company, founded in 1602, played a central role in the colonization of the East Indies, establishing trading posts, forts, and plantations throughout the archipelago.

The Dutch presence in Indonesia had profound social, economic, and cultural implications for the region. Dutch colonial rule brought about significant changes in governance, with the establishment of a highly centralized administration and the imposition of Dutch legal and educational systems.

The Dutch also introduced cash crops such as coffee, tea, and rubber, transforming the agricultural landscape and fueling economic growth. However, these economic policies often came at the expense of indigenous communities, who were subjected to forced labor, land confiscation, and other forms of exploitation.

The Dutch East Indies also became a melting pot of cultures, with the intermingling of Dutch, Indonesian, Chinese, and other ethnic groups giving rise to a rich tapestry of languages, religions, and traditions. Despite efforts by the Dutch colonial authorities to impose cultural assimilation, indigenous customs and beliefs remained resilient, contributing to the diverse cultural mosaic of modern-day Indonesia.

In addition to the East Indies, the Netherlands also established colonies in other parts of Asia, including present-day Sri Lanka, Taiwan, and India. These colonies served as strategic outposts for Dutch trade and commerce, enabling the Netherlands to compete with other European powers for dominance in the region.

In Africa, the Dutch established a foothold in the Cape Colony, located in present-day South Africa, where they established a settlement at Cape Town in 1652. The Cape Colony became a crucial stopover point for Dutch ships en route to the East Indies, and the Dutch East India Company played a significant role in the colonization and development of the region.

The legacy of Dutch colonialism in South Africa is complex, marked by both cooperation and conflict with indigenous Khoikhoi and San peoples, as well as later clashes with British colonial forces. The Dutch settlers, known as Boers or Afrikaners, played a central role in the establishment of apartheid, a system of racial segregation that would define South African society for much of the 20th century.

In the Americas, the Dutch established colonies in what is now New York, Suriname, and the Dutch Caribbean islands. In New Netherland, as the Dutch colony in North America was known, Dutch settlers established trading posts and agricultural settlements, laying the groundwork for the multicultural society that would eventually emerge in the United States.

In Suriname and the Dutch Caribbean, the Dutch established sugar plantations worked by enslaved Africans, contributing to the wealth and prosperity of the Dutch Republic. The legacy of slavery and colonialism continues to shape the social, economic, and political landscape of these regions today, with ongoing debates about reparations, reconciliation, and historical memory.

In summary, the Dutch colonial legacy is a complex and multifaceted phenomenon that continues to reverberate across the globe. From Indonesia to South Africa, the Americas to the Caribbean, the impact of Dutch colonialism is still felt in the cultural, social, and economic dynamics of former colonial territories.

The Rise of the Dutch Republic

The rise of the Dutch Republic marks a pivotal period in Dutch history, characterized by the struggle for independence from Spanish rule and the emergence of a new political and economic order in the Low Countries. The seeds of rebellion were sown in the 16th century, as the Netherlands, then part of the Spanish Habsburg Empire, chafed under the authoritarian rule of King Philip II.

Tensions reached a boiling point with the imposition of religious persecution against Protestant dissenters, leading to widespread unrest and resistance among the Dutch populace. In 1566, a wave of iconoclasm swept across the Netherlands, as Calvinist mobs attacked Catholic churches and religious symbols in protest against Spanish tyranny.

In response to the growing unrest, King Philip II dispatched his most trusted general, the Duke of Alba, to crush the rebellion and restore order. Alba's brutal crackdown, known as the "Council of Blood," resulted in the execution of thousands of suspected rebels and the imposition of harsh martial law.

Despite the repression, the Dutch resistance persisted, fueled by a potent mix of religious fervor, economic grievances, and nationalist sentiment. In 1568, William of Orange, a Dutch nobleman and leader of the resistance, launched a full-scale revolt against Spanish rule, sparking the Eighty Years' War.

The early years of the revolt were marked by setbacks and defeats for the Dutch rebels, as Spanish forces under the command of the Duke of Parma gained the upper hand on the battlefield. However, the tide began to turn in favor of the Dutch with the arrival of foreign support, including financial backing from England and military assistance from Protestant princes in Germany.

In 1579, the northern provinces of the Netherlands, led by Holland and Zeeland, formally declared their independence from Spain in the Union of Utrecht, laying the foundation for the Dutch Republic. The southern provinces, meanwhile, remained under Spanish control, eventually becoming part of present-day Belgium.

The Dutch Republic emerged as a unique experiment in republican government, with power vested in the hands of a wealthy merchant class known as the regents. The Republic adopted a decentralized system of governance, with each province retaining considerable autonomy while cooperating on matters of mutual interest through the States General, a national assembly.

The Dutch Golden Age, spanning the 17th century, saw the Republic rise to prominence as a global trading power, with Amsterdam emerging as the financial capital of Europe. Dutch merchants established extensive trading networks spanning the globe, from the Baltic Sea to the East Indies, fueling an unprecedented era of economic growth and prosperity.

The Dutch Republic also became a center of artistic and intellectual innovation, with painters such as Rembrandt van Rijn and Johannes Vermeer producing masterpieces that continue to captivate audiences to this day. The Republic's commitment to religious tolerance and freedom of expression attracted persecuted groups from across Europe, including Sephardic Jews and Huguenot refugees.

Despite its remarkable achievements, the Dutch Republic faced numerous challenges, including internal divisions, external threats from rival European powers, and economic downturns. In 1672, the Republic was plunged into crisis with the outbreak of the Franco-Dutch War and the invasion of the Netherlands by France and its allies, leading to a period of political upheaval known as the "Disaster Year."

However, the Dutch Republic managed to weather the storm, emerging from the turmoil with its independence and sovereignty intact. Though the Republic would eventually decline in the face of internal strife and external pressures, its legacy as a beacon of freedom, tolerance, and prosperity continues to inspire generations of Dutch people and admirers around the world.

Golden Age: Dutch Trade, Art, and Innovation

The Golden Age of the Netherlands, spanning the 17th century, was a period of unprecedented prosperity, cultural flourishing, and innovation. At the heart of this golden era was Dutch trade, which fueled the country's economic growth and global influence. Dutch merchants established extensive trading networks that spanned the globe, from the Baltic Sea to the East Indies, importing spices, textiles, and luxury goods from Asia and exporting Dutch manufactured goods such as textiles, ceramics, and firearms.

Central to the success of Dutch trade was the Dutch East India Company (VOC), founded in 1602 as the world's first multinational corporation. The VOC dominated trade with Asia, establishing fortified trading posts and monopolies on key commodities such as spices, tea, and porcelain. The profits from VOC trade flowed back to the Netherlands, enriching merchants and investors and fueling further economic expansion.

The Dutch Republic emerged as the financial capital of Europe, with Amsterdam serving as the hub of international commerce and finance. The Amsterdam Stock Exchange, founded in 1602, was the world's first official stock exchange, providing a platform for investors to buy and sell shares in VOC and other companies. The Dutch banking system, characterized by innovative financial instruments such as bills of exchange and marine insurance, facilitated the flow of capital and investment.

The economic prosperity of the Golden Age paved the way for a cultural renaissance, as Dutch artists, writers, and thinkers flourished in an atmosphere of freedom, tolerance, and creativity. Dutch painting reached its zenith during this period, with artists such as Rembrandt van Rijn, Johannes Vermeer, and Frans Hals producing masterpieces that captured the richness and complexity of Dutch society.

Rembrandt, in particular, is celebrated for his mastery of light and shadow, as well as his ability to capture the humanity and emotion of his subjects. His iconic works, such as "The Night Watch" and "The Anatomy Lesson of Dr. Nicolaes Tulp," continue to inspire awe and admiration.

Vermeer, meanwhile, is renowned for his exquisite depiction of everyday life, with works such as "Girl with a Pearl Earring" and "The Milkmaid" exemplifying his mastery of color, composition, and atmosphere.

In addition to painting, the Golden Age saw remarkable achievements in other fields of art and culture, including literature, music, and architecture. Dutch literature flourished with the works of writers such as Joost van den Vondel and Pieter Corneliszoon Hooft, while Dutch composers such as Jan Pieterszoon Sweelinck and Jacob van Eyck made significant contributions to the development of European music.

Dutch architecture also experienced a golden age, with the construction of grand civic buildings, merchant houses, and canal houses that continue to define the urban landscape of Dutch cities such as Amsterdam, Haarlem, and Utrecht.

Innovation was another hallmark of the Golden Age, with Dutch scientists, engineers, and inventors making significant contributions to fields such as cartography, navigation, and hydraulic engineering. Willem Janszoon Blaeu and his son Joan Blaeu produced some of the most accurate and detailed maps of the period, while Antonie van Leeuwenhoek made pioneering discoveries in microscopy and microbiology.

The legacy of the Golden Age continues to shape Dutch identity and culture to this day, with its achievements in trade, art, and innovation serving as a source of national pride and inspiration. From the canals of Amsterdam to the masterpieces of Rembrandt, the Golden Age remains a testament to the ingenuity, creativity, and resilience of the Dutch people.

The Dutch East India Company: A Maritime Empire

The Dutch East India Company (Vereenigde Oost-Indische Compagnie or VOC) stands as a testament to the height of Dutch maritime power and commercial ambition during the 17th and 18th centuries. Established in 1602, the VOC was the world's first multinational corporation, with a mandate from the Dutch government to conduct trade in Asia. Its primary goal was to dominate the spice trade, particularly in the lucrative markets of the East Indies, which encompassed present-day Indonesia, Malaysia, and parts of India and Sri Lanka.

The VOC operated as a state-sponsored enterprise, with exclusive rights to trade with Asia granted by the Dutch government. It was granted expansive powers, including the ability to establish colonies, mint currency, wage war, and negotiate treaties with indigenous rulers. This unique combination of private enterprise and state authority enabled the VOC to become one of the most powerful and influential trading companies in history.

The VOC's trading network spanned the globe, with operations extending from the Cape of Good Hope in South Africa to Nagasaki in Japan. Its fleet of merchant ships, armed with cannons and manned by skilled sailors and soldiers, traversed treacherous seas to reach the spice-rich islands of the East Indies. These voyages were fraught with peril, as

Dutch ships faced the threat of pirates, storms, and rival European powers vying for control of Asian trade routes.

To protect its interests and maintain its monopoly on the spice trade, the VOC established fortified trading posts and colonies throughout the East Indies. These settlements served as centers of commerce, administration, and defense, allowing the VOC to control the production, processing, and distribution of spices such as cloves, nutmeg, and pepper.

The VOC's dominance in the spice trade was not without controversy, as its operations often involved coercion, exploitation, and violence. Indigenous peoples were subjected to forced labor, land confiscation, and harsh treatment, while rival European traders were driven out or forced to pay exorbitant taxes and fees.

Despite these ethical concerns, the VOC's trade with Asia brought immense wealth and prosperity to the Dutch Republic, contributing to its status as the financial capital of Europe during the Golden Age. The profits from VOC trade financed Dutch art, culture, and science, as well as the construction of grand civic buildings, canal houses, and merchant mansions in cities like Amsterdam and Rotterdam.

The VOC's influence extended beyond trade to encompass diplomacy, exploration, and cultural exchange. Dutch sailors and explorers, sponsored by the VOC, charted uncharted waters, mapped unknown lands, and made groundbreaking discoveries in geography, astronomy, and natural history. Figures such as Willem Janszoon, Abel Tasman, and Jan Pieterszoon Coen became legendary for their exploits in the service of the VOC.

However, the VOC's success was not without its challenges, as competition from rival European powers, internal corruption, and mismanagement eventually led to its decline. In 1799, after nearly two centuries of operation, the VOC was dissolved by the Dutch government, bringing an end to its reign as a maritime empire.

Nevertheless, the legacy of the Dutch East India Company lives on, as its achievements in trade, exploration, and colonization continue to shape the modern world. From the spices of the East Indies to the cultural exchange between East and West, the VOC's impact is felt in the global economy, politics, and culture to this day.

World Wars and Dutch Resistance

The World Wars brought unprecedented challenges and upheaval to the Netherlands, testing the resilience and courage of its people in the face of adversity. During World War I, the Netherlands managed to maintain its neutrality, avoiding direct involvement in the conflict that ravaged much of Europe. However, the war had profound economic and social repercussions for the country, as trade disruptions and shortages led to widespread hardship and discontent among the Dutch populace.

The interwar period saw the rise of political extremism and growing tensions in Europe, foreshadowing the looming threat of another global conflict. In May 1940, Nazi Germany invaded the Netherlands as part of its Blitzkrieg campaign to conquer Western Europe. Despite putting up fierce resistance, Dutch forces were overwhelmed by the superior firepower and tactics of the German army, and the Netherlands fell under Nazi occupation.

The German occupation of the Netherlands brought hardship and suffering to the Dutch people, as they endured food shortages, forced labor, and repression under the brutal rule of the Nazi regime. The Dutch government, led by Queen Wilhelmina, went into exile in London, where it continued to resist the German occupation and support the Allied war effort.

Despite the risks, many ordinary Dutch citizens chose to resist the Nazi occupiers in various ways, forming underground networks, publishing clandestine newspapers, and sheltering Jews and other persecuted groups from persecution. The Dutch Resistance, as it came to be known, played a crucial role in sabotaging German operations, gathering intelligence, and providing aid to Allied soldiers and downed pilots.

One of the most famous acts of Dutch resistance occurred in February 1941, when a group of Dutch Communist Party members and trade unionists staged a strike in Amsterdam to protest the persecution of Jews. The strike, known as the February Strike, was brutally suppressed by the German authorities, but it served as a powerful symbol of Dutch resistance and solidarity in the face of Nazi oppression.

The Dutch Resistance was not without risk, as resistance members faced arrest, torture, and execution by the Gestapo and other Nazi security forces. Despite the dangers, thousands of Dutch men and women chose to join the resistance movement, motivated by a deep sense of patriotism and a commitment to freedom and justice.

The Dutch Resistance also played a crucial role in helping Jews evade deportation to Nazi concentration camps. Many Dutch families risked their lives to hide Jews in their homes, attics, and basements, providing them with food, clothing, and false identity papers. The efforts of these brave individuals saved thousands of Jewish lives during the Holocaust.

The Dutch Resistance continued to operate throughout the war, even as the tide began to turn against the Nazis and Allied forces launched the liberation of Europe. In May 1945, following the surrender of Nazi Germany, the Netherlands was finally liberated from German occupation, bringing an end to five years of hardship and suffering.

The legacy of the Dutch Resistance lives on as a symbol of courage, sacrifice, and solidarity in the face of tyranny and oppression. The men and women who risked their lives to resist Nazi occupation are honored as heroes in the Netherlands and serve as a reminder of the importance of standing up for freedom and human rights, even in the darkest of times.

Modern Netherlands: A Progressive Society

In the modern era, the Netherlands has earned a reputation as a progressive and forward-thinking society, known for its commitment to social welfare, environmental sustainability, and human rights. With a population known for its tolerance, openness, and pragmatism, the Netherlands has embraced diversity and inclusion as core values, striving to create a society where everyone can thrive.

One of the hallmarks of modern Dutch society is its robust social welfare system, which provides comprehensive healthcare, education, and social services to all citizens. The Netherlands boasts one of the highest standards of living in the world, with low levels of poverty, unemployment, and income inequality. Its universal healthcare system ensures that everyone has access to quality medical care, while its education system emphasizes inclusivity, innovation, and lifelong learning.

The Netherlands is also a pioneer in environmental sustainability, with a strong commitment to renewable energy, conservation, and climate action. Dutch cities are renowned for their bike-friendly infrastructure, efficient public transportation, and sustainable urban planning, making them among the greenest and most livable cities in the world. The Dutch government has set ambitious targets to reduce greenhouse gas emissions, promote renewable energy sources, and protect natural habitats, leading the way in the global fight against climate change. In addition to its progressive policies on healthcare and the environment, the Netherlands is also a champion of human rights and social justice. The country has a long history of advocating for LGBTQ+ rights, gender equality, and minority rights, with laws and policies in place to protect the rights and dignity of all citizens. Same-sex marriage has been legal in the Netherlands since 2001, making it one of the first countries in the world to recognize marriage equality.

The Netherlands is also known for its innovative approach to governance and public policy, with a tradition of consensus-based decision-making and pragmatic problem-solving. Dutch politicians and policymakers prioritize evidence-based solutions, stakeholder engagement, and compromise, seeking to find common ground and build consensus on issues ranging from healthcare reform to immigration policy.

Despite its progressive reputation, the Netherlands faces challenges and debates on issues such as immigration, multiculturalism, and the future of the European Union. Like many countries in Europe, the Netherlands grapples with questions of identity, integration, and national sovereignty in an increasingly interconnected and diverse world.

Nevertheless, the Netherlands remains committed to its values of tolerance, openness, and solidarity, seeking to build a society where everyone has the opportunity to fulfill their potential and contribute to the common good. In an era of uncertainty and change, the Netherlands stands as a beacon of hope and inspiration, demonstrating that progress and prosperity can go hand in hand with compassion and social justice.

Dutch Monarchy: Tradition and Evolution

The Dutch monarchy has a long and storied history, rooted in centuries of tradition and evolution. The modern Dutch monarchy traces its origins back to the House of Orange-Nassau, which rose to prominence in the 16th century as leaders of the Dutch Revolt against Spanish rule. William of Orange, also known as William the Silent, became the first stadtholder of the Dutch Republic and is regarded as the founder of the Dutch monarchy.

The Dutch monarchy underwent significant changes during the French Revolutionary and Napoleonic Wars, when the Netherlands was occupied by French forces and transformed into the Batavian Republic, a client state of France. After the defeat of Napoleon, the Congress of Vienna established the United Kingdom of the Netherlands in 1815, with William of Orange becoming King William I. The modern Dutch monarchy took shape in 1848 with the adoption of a new constitution that transformed the Netherlands into a constitutional monarchy, limiting the powers of the monarch and establishing a parliamentary system of government. Since then, the Dutch monarch has served as a ceremonial head of state, with executive authority vested in the government and prime minister.

The House of Orange-Nassau has played a central role in Dutch politics and society, with members of the royal family serving as symbols of national unity and continuity. Queen Wilhelmina, who reigned from 1890 to 1948, was a beloved figure during World War II, leading the Dutch government in exile and inspiring the Dutch resistance against Nazi occupation. In recent decades, the Dutch monarchy has undergone a process of modernization and adaptation to changing social norms and expectations. Queen Beatrix, who reigned from 1980 to 2013, abdicated in favor of her son, Willem-Alexander, in 2013, marking the first male monarch in over a century.

King Willem-Alexander and his wife, Queen Máxima, have embraced their roles with enthusiasm and dedication, undertaking numerous official duties and engagements at home and abroad. They are actively involved in promoting Dutch trade and diplomacy, as well as championing causes such as water management, sustainability, and mental health awareness.

The Dutch monarchy remains popular and respected in the Netherlands, with members of the royal family enjoying widespread support and affection from the Dutch people. The monarchy serves as a unifying force in Dutch society, transcending political divides and fostering a sense of national identity and pride.

Despite its ceremonial nature, the Dutch monarchy continues to evolve in response to changing social, political, and cultural dynamics. The royal family strives to remain relevant and accessible to the Dutch people, while upholding the traditions and values that have defined the Dutch monarchy for centuries. As the Netherlands enters a new era of globalization and uncertainty, the monarchy remains a symbol of stability, continuity, and national unity.

Dutch Democracy: Institutions and Governance

Dutch democracy is characterized by a robust system of institutions and governance that has evolved over centuries to reflect the values of pluralism, participation, and accountability. At its core is a parliamentary democracy, where sovereignty is vested in the people and exercised through elected representatives in the Dutch Parliament, known as the Staten-Generaal.

The Dutch Parliament consists of two chambers: the House of Representatives (Tweede Kamer) and the Senate (Eerste Kamer). Members of the House of Representatives are elected by proportional representation in national elections held every four years, while members of the Senate are chosen by the members of the provincial legislatures. The Parliament is responsible for making laws, approving the national budget, and overseeing the government's policies and actions.

The Dutch government is led by the Prime Minister, who is appointed by the monarch and is usually the leader of the political party that holds the most seats in the House of Representatives. The Prime Minister heads the Council of Ministers, which is composed of ministers responsible for different government departments. The government is responsible for implementing laws, managing the country's affairs, and representing the Netherlands in international relations.

In addition to the Parliament and government, the Netherlands has a system of decentralized governance, with authority and responsibilities divided between the central government and the regional and local authorities. The country is divided into twelve provinces, each with its own elected provincial council and executive board responsible for regional matters such as infrastructure, education, and culture. Below the provincial level are municipalities, which have their own elected councils and mayors and are responsible for local services and administration.

The Dutch legal system is based on civil law and is characterized by its independence, impartiality, and accessibility. The judiciary is composed of independent courts that adjudicate disputes, interpret laws, and uphold the rule of law. The highest court in the Netherlands is the Supreme Court, which has the authority to review decisions of lower courts and ensure the uniform application of the law.

Dutch democracy is also characterized by a strong tradition of political participation and civic engagement. Political parties play a central role in the democratic process, with a wide range of parties representing diverse interests and ideologies. Elections are free, fair, and competitive, with high levels of voter turnout and engagement.

The Dutch political system is known for its consensus-oriented approach, with politicians and policymakers seeking to build broad coalitions and find common ground on issues of national importance. This culture of compromise and cooperation has contributed to the stability and effectiveness of Dutch governance, enabling the country to address complex challenges and adapt to changing circumstances.

Overall, Dutch democracy is a dynamic and resilient system that continues to evolve in response to internal and external pressures. By upholding the principles of democracy, rule of law, and respect for human rights, the Netherlands remains a model of good governance and democratic governance for countries around the world.

Amsterdam: A City of Canals and Culture

Amsterdam, the capital city of the Netherlands, is a vibrant metropolis known for its picturesque canals, rich history, and diverse cultural scene. Situated in the western part of the country, Amsterdam is home to over 800,000 residents and attracts millions of visitors from around the world each year.

One of the most iconic features of Amsterdam is its extensive network of canals, which crisscross the city like arteries, giving it the nickname "Venice of the North." The canals, which date back to the 17th century, were originally built for transportation, defense, and water management and are now a UNESCO World Heritage Site. Visitors can explore Amsterdam's waterways by boat, bike, or on foot, admiring the elegant canal houses, picturesque bridges, and historic landmarks that line the waterfront.

Amsterdam's rich history is evident in its well-preserved architecture, which spans centuries and reflects a variety of architectural styles, from medieval churches and Renaissance palaces to modernist buildings and cutting-edge contemporary designs. The city's historic center, known as the Grachtengordel, is a labyrinth of narrow streets, charming squares, and hidden courtyards, where visitors can wander and discover hidden gems around every corner.

In addition to its architectural heritage, Amsterdam is renowned for its world-class museums and cultural institutions. The Rijksmuseum, located on Museumplein, is home to an extensive collection of Dutch masterpieces, including works by Rembrandt, Vermeer, and Van Gogh. The Van Gogh Museum, dedicated to the life and work of the legendary Dutch painter, is another must-visit destination for art lovers.

Amsterdam's cultural scene is also vibrant and diverse, with a thriving music, theater, and nightlife scene that caters to all tastes and interests. The city is home to numerous theaters, concert halls, and music venues, where visitors can enjoy everything from classical concerts and opera performances to cutting-edge electronic music and experimental theater.

Amsterdam is also known for its progressive and liberal attitudes, with a long history of tolerance and acceptance. The city's famous Red Light District, located in the De Wallen neighborhood, is a prime example of Amsterdam's open-minded approach to controversial issues such as sex work and drug policy. While the Red Light District may be a magnet for tourists, it is also a symbol of Amsterdam's commitment to individual freedom and personal choice.

In recent years, Amsterdam has emerged as a global hub for technology, innovation, and entrepreneurship, attracting startups, tech companies, and creative professionals from around the world. The city's thriving startup ecosystem, vibrant coworking spaces, and supportive business climate have made it an attractive destination for aspiring entrepreneurs and innovators looking to launch their own ventures.

Despite its modernization and cosmopolitan character, Amsterdam has managed to retain its unique charm and character, with its picturesque canals, historic landmarks, and laid-back atmosphere attracting visitors of all ages and backgrounds. Whether exploring the city's cultural treasures, cruising along its canals, or simply soaking up the atmosphere at a cozy café, Amsterdam offers something for everyone to enjoy and discover.

Rotterdam: Europe's Largest Port City

Rotterdam, often referred to as the "Gateway to Europe," is Europe's largest port city and a bustling hub of maritime activity and international trade. Situated in the southwestern part of the Netherlands, Rotterdam occupies a strategic location at the mouth of the Rhine River, making it an ideal gateway for goods entering and leaving Europe.

The Port of Rotterdam is the largest port in Europe and one of the busiest in the world, handling millions of tons of cargo each year, including containers, oil, chemicals, and bulk goods. The port is a vital link in the global supply chain, connecting Europe to markets around the world and facilitating trade between continents.

The Port of Rotterdam is not just a transportation hub but also a major industrial center, with numerous refineries, petrochemical plants, and manufacturing facilities located within its boundaries. The port's strategic location and state-of-the-art infrastructure make it an attractive destination for businesses looking to establish a presence in Europe.

In addition to its industrial and commercial importance, Rotterdam is also a vibrant cultural and architectural center, known for its bold modernist architecture, innovative urban design, and dynamic arts scene. The city's skyline is dominated by striking skyscrapers, such as the iconic Erasmus Bridge, the Euromast tower, and the De Rotterdam building, designed by renowned architects such as Rem Koolhaas and Piet Blom.

Rotterdam's cultural offerings are diverse and eclectic, with world-class museums, galleries, and cultural institutions that showcase the city's rich history and vibrant contemporary art scene. The Kunsthal Rotterdam, the Boijmans Van Beuningen Museum, and the Netherlands Architecture Institute are just a few of the city's cultural highlights, attracting visitors from around the world.

Despite its modernization and cosmopolitan character, Rotterdam has managed to preserve its historic charm and character, with picturesque canals, historic neighborhoods, and charming waterfronts that offer a glimpse into the city's storied past. The Old Harbor area, known as Delfshaven, is a prime example of Rotterdam's maritime heritage, with its well-preserved historic buildings, traditional Dutch ships, and cozy cafes and restaurants.

Rotterdam's transformation from a war-torn city to a thriving metropolis is a testament to its resilience, innovation, and entrepreneurial spirit. Following the devastation of World War II, Rotterdam embarked on a bold reconstruction effort that reshaped the city's landscape and laid the foundation for its future growth and prosperity.

Today, Rotterdam is a dynamic and forward-thinking city that continues to evolve and reinvent itself, embracing new technologies, sustainability initiatives, and urban development projects that position it as a leader in the 21st-century global economy. With its world-class port facilities, vibrant cultural scene, and innovative spirit, Rotterdam is poised to remain a key player on the international stage for years to come.

The Hague: International City of Peace and Justice

The Hague, known as Den Haag in Dutch, is a city of great significance on the international stage, renowned as the political and administrative capital of the Netherlands. Situated along the western coast of the country, The Hague is home to numerous international organizations, diplomatic missions, and institutions dedicated to peace, justice, and human rights.

One of the most prominent institutions in The Hague is the International Court of Justice (ICJ), often referred to as the World Court. Established in 1945, the ICJ is the principal judicial organ of the United Nations, tasked with settling disputes between states and providing advisory opinions on legal questions referred by UN bodies and specialized agencies. The ICJ's imposing Peace Palace, built in 1913, serves as a symbol of international cooperation and the pursuit of justice.

In addition to the ICJ, The Hague is also home to the International Criminal Court (ICC), the first permanent international court established to prosecute individuals for genocide, war crimes, crimes against humanity, and aggression. The ICC, which began operating in 2002, plays a crucial role in holding perpetrators of grave international crimes accountable and delivering justice to victims around the world.

The Hague is further distinguished as the seat of numerous international organizations and tribunals, including the International Criminal Tribunal for the former Yugoslavia (ICTY), the International Residual Mechanism for Criminal Tribunals (IRMCT), and the Special Tribunal for Lebanon (STL). These institutions play a vital role in addressing impunity for serious international crimes and promoting the rule of law and respect for human rights.

Beyond its role as a center for international law and justice, The Hague is also a vibrant and cosmopolitan city with a rich cultural heritage and diverse population. The city boasts numerous museums, art galleries, and cultural institutions that celebrate its history, art, and culture. The Mauritshuis, home to masterpieces by Vermeer, Rembrandt, and other Dutch masters, is a must-visit destination for art enthusiasts.

The Hague's historic city center, with its stately mansions, elegant squares, and leafy parks, exudes an air of grandeur and sophistication, while its bustling streets and lively neighborhoods offer a glimpse into everyday life in the Netherlands. Visitors can explore the picturesque Binnenhof, the oldest parliament building in the world still in use, or stroll along the seaside promenade of Scheveningen, a popular beach resort.

The Hague's reputation as an international city of peace and justice is further enhanced by its commitment to sustainability, innovation, and social justice. The city is a leader in environmental sustainability, with ambitious plans to reduce carbon emissions, promote renewable energy, and enhance green spaces. It is also a hub for innovation and technology, with a thriving startup ecosystem and numerous initiatives aimed at fostering entrepreneurship and creativity.

In summary, The Hague stands as a beacon of hope and inspiration on the international stage, embodying the values of peace, justice, and cooperation. With its impressive array of international institutions, vibrant cultural scene, and commitment to sustainability and innovation, The Hague continues to play a leading role in shaping the future of the Netherlands and the world.

Utrecht: The Heart of the Netherlands

Utrecht, often referred to as the "Heart of the Netherlands," is a city steeped in history, culture, and innovation. Situated in the central part of the country, Utrecht is one of the oldest cities in the Netherlands, with a history dating back over 2,000 years. It was founded by the Romans around 50 CE and has since grown into a dynamic and vibrant urban center.

One of Utrecht's most distinctive features is its medieval city center, characterized by narrow cobblestone streets, historic buildings, and picturesque canals. The iconic Dom Tower, standing at 112 meters tall, dominates the skyline and serves as a symbol of the city's rich architectural heritage. Visitors can climb to the top of the tower for panoramic views of the city and surrounding countryside.

Utrecht is also known for its thriving cultural scene, with numerous museums, galleries, and theaters that showcase the city's artistic and creative talents. The Centraal Museum, housed in a former medieval monastery, is home to a diverse collection of art, artifacts, and historical objects that tell the story of Utrecht's past and present. The city's theaters, such as the Stadsschouwburg Utrecht and TivoliVredenburg, host a wide range of performances, from classical concerts and opera to contemporary theater and dance.

In addition to its cultural offerings, Utrecht is a center of education and innovation, with one of the largest universities in the Netherlands, Utrecht University, located in the city. The university, founded in 1636, is renowned for its research and academic excellence, particularly in fields such as science, medicine, and law. Utrecht is also home to numerous research institutes, tech startups, and incubators that drive innovation and economic growth in the region.

Utrecht's central location makes it a key transportation hub and economic center in the Netherlands. The city is served by an extensive network of trains, buses, and trams, making it easy to travel to and from other major cities in the country. Utrecht's central railway station, one of the busiest in the Netherlands, connects the city to destinations across Europe, making it a popular choice for commuters and travelers alike.

Despite its modern amenities and cosmopolitan character, Utrecht has managed to retain its small-town charm and sense of community. The city's neighborhoods are known for their lively street markets, cozy cafes, and vibrant public squares, where residents gather to socialize, shop, and relax. Utrecht's strong sense of community is evident in its numerous festivals, events, and traditions that bring people together and celebrate the city's unique identity.

In summary, Utrecht is much more than just a geographical center of the Netherlands—it is the beating heart of the country, pulsating with history, culture, and innovation. With its rich architectural heritage, dynamic cultural scene, and spirit of creativity and entrepreneurship, Utrecht continues to captivate and inspire visitors from around the world.

Groningen: University Town and Cultural Hub

Groningen, nestled in the northeastern region of the Netherlands, is a vibrant university town and cultural hub brimming with energy and creativity. Home to the University of Groningen, one of the oldest and most prestigious universities in the country, the city has a youthful and dynamic atmosphere, with students comprising a significant portion of its population.

The University of Groningen, founded in 1614, is renowned for its academic excellence and research prowess, particularly in fields such as science, medicine, and humanities. With over 30,000 students from diverse backgrounds and disciplines, the university fosters a stimulating intellectual environment that attracts scholars and researchers from around the world.

Groningen's status as a university town has had a profound impact on its cultural scene, with numerous theaters, art galleries, and music venues that cater to the city's vibrant student population. The Groninger Museum, with its striking modernist architecture and eclectic collection of art and artifacts, is a must-visit destination for art enthusiasts.

The city's historic center, with its charming cobblestone streets, medieval buildings, and lively squares, is a testament to Groningen's rich history and architectural heritage. The Martinitoren, or Martini Tower, is a prominent landmark that offers panoramic views of the city and surrounding countryside. Visitors can also explore the centuries-old Groninger Museum, located in the heart of the city, which houses an impressive collection of art and artifacts spanning centuries. Groningen's cultural offerings extend beyond its museums and galleries to include a vibrant music scene, with numerous festivals, concerts, and performances held throughout the year. The annual Eurosonic Noorderslag festival, held in January, showcases up-and-coming musical talent from across Europe and attracts thousands of music fans to the city. In addition to its cultural attractions, Groningen is also known for its green spaces and outdoor recreational opportunities. The city boasts numerous parks, gardens, and nature reserves where residents and visitors can enjoy walking, cycling, and picnicking. The Noorderplantsoen, a large park located in the heart of the city, is a popular destination for outdoor activities and social gatherings.

Groningen's central location in the northern part of the Netherlands makes it an important transportation hub and economic center for the region. The city is well-connected by road, rail, and water, with excellent transportation links to other major cities in the country and beyond.

Despite its modern amenities and cosmopolitan character, Groningen has managed to retain its small-town charm and sense of community. The city's neighborhoods are known for their friendly atmosphere, vibrant street life, and strong sense of identity. Whether exploring its historic landmarks, attending a cultural event, or simply soaking up the atmosphere at a cozy cafe, Groningen offers something for everyone to enjoy and discover.

Dutch Language: History, Structure, and Usage

The Dutch language, also known as Nederlands, is a West Germanic language spoken by over 23 million people worldwide, primarily in the Netherlands, Belgium, Suriname, and parts of the Caribbean. It is closely related to other Germanic languages such as German and English, sharing many similarities in vocabulary, grammar, and syntax.

The history of the Dutch language can be traced back to the early Middle Ages, when it emerged as a distinct language from the Frankish dialects spoken in the region. Over time, Dutch evolved through contact with other languages, including Latin, French, and Low German, resulting in the development of a rich and diverse linguistic heritage.

The structure of the Dutch language is characterized by its use of grammatical gender, with nouns classified as either masculine, feminine, or neuter. Dutch nouns also have a system of grammatical case, with different forms used for subjects, objects, and possessives. Verbs in Dutch are conjugated according to tense, mood, and aspect, with regular and irregular forms.

Dutch is known for its relatively simple phonology, with a fairly small inventory of vowel and consonant sounds compared to other languages. However, it does have some unique features, such as the presence of guttural sounds like the "g" in "gezellig" and the "ch" in "acht." Dutch spelling is largely phonetic, meaning that words are spelled the way they are pronounced, although there are some irregularities and exceptions. In terms of usage, Dutch is the official language of the Netherlands and Belgium, where it is used in government, education, media, and everyday communication. It is also widely spoken as a second language in many former Dutch colonies, such as Suriname, Aruba, and Curacao, as well as in immigrant communities around the world.

Dutch has a rich literary tradition, with a long history of poetry, prose, and drama dating back to the Middle Ages. Some of the most famous Dutch writers include Joost van den Vondel, considered the greatest Dutch poet of the 17th century, and Multatuli, whose novel "Max Havelaar" is regarded as a masterpiece of Dutch literature.

In recent years, Dutch has become increasingly important as a global language of commerce, science, and technology, with many multinational companies and organizations conducting business in Dutch-speaking countries. As a result, there has been a growing demand for Dutch language education and proficiency testing, both within the Netherlands and abroad.

Despite the influence of globalization and the spread of English as a lingua franca, Dutch remains a vibrant and dynamic language with a strong sense of identity and cultural pride. Whether spoken on the streets of Amsterdam, in the halls of the Dutch Parliament, or in the classrooms of Dutch schools, the Dutch language continues to play a central role in shaping the collective identity and heritage of the Dutch-speaking world.

Dutch Cuisine: From Stroopwafels to Stamppot

Dutch cuisine is a delightful fusion of flavors and traditions, reflecting the country's rich agricultural heritage and maritime influences. From hearty comfort foods to sweet treats, Dutch cuisine offers a diverse array of dishes that are sure to tantalize the taste buds.

One of the most iconic Dutch foods is stroopwafels, thin waffle cookies filled with caramel syrup. These sweet treats are a favorite snack among locals and visitors alike, often enjoyed with a cup of coffee or tea. Stroopwafels are believed to have originated in the city of Gouda in the late 18th century and have since become a beloved Dutch delicacy.

Another popular Dutch dish is stamppot, a hearty comfort food made with mashed potatoes mixed with vegetables such as kale, sauerkraut, or carrots. Stamppot is often served with a savory meat such as rookworst, a smoked sausage, and topped with gravy or mustard. This comforting dish is a staple of Dutch cuisine, especially during the colder months.

Herring is another traditional Dutch delicacy that has been enjoyed for centuries. Raw herring, known as haring, is typically served with onions and pickles and eaten whole by holding it by the tail and taking a bite. While raw herring may not be to everyone's taste, it is a beloved street food in the Netherlands, especially during the herring season in the spring. Dutch cheese is world-famous, with varieties such as Gouda, Edam, and Leiden being exported around the globe. Gouda cheese, named after the city where it was originally traded, is a semi-hard cheese with a rich, buttery flavor. Edam cheese, known for its distinctive round shape and red wax coating, is slightly milder in flavor and is often used in sandwiches and salads. Dutch pancakes, known as pannenkoeken, are a beloved breakfast or dessert option in the Netherlands. These thin, crepe-like pancakes can be served sweet or savory, with toppings such as powdered sugar, syrup, fruit, cheese, or bacon. Pannenkoeken houses, or pancake houses, are popular dining destinations where diners can enjoy a wide variety of pancake creations.

Bitterballen are a popular Dutch snack, consisting of deep-fried balls of meat ragout coated in breadcrumbs. These savory treats are often served as appetizers or bar snacks, accompanied by mustard for dipping. Bitterballen are a quintessential part of Dutch cuisine and are enjoyed by locals and tourists alike.

Dutch cuisine also includes a variety of delicious pastries and baked goods, such as oliebollen, or Dutch donuts, which are traditionally eaten on New Year's Eve. These deep-fried dough balls are dusted with powdered sugar and can be filled with raisins, currants, or chopped apples. Another popular pastry is appeltaart, or Dutch apple pie, made with a buttery crust and filled with cinnamon-spiced apples.

Overall, Dutch cuisine is a delightful blend of flavors, textures, and traditions that reflect the country's rich culinary heritage. Whether indulging in a savory stamppot, savoring a sweet stroopwafel, or enjoying a crispy bitterbal, Dutch food offers something for every palate to enjoy.

Dutch Wildlife: Exploring the Natural Kingdom

Dutch wildlife offers a fascinating glimpse into the natural kingdom of the Netherlands, a country known for its diverse landscapes and unique ecosystems. Despite its small size and heavily populated urban areas, the Netherlands is home to a surprising variety of plant and animal species, many of which are adapted to its wetlands, forests, and coastal habitats.

One of the most iconic symbols of Dutch wildlife is the European hare, a common sight in the countryside and agricultural areas. These fast-running mammals are known for their long ears and powerful hind legs, which enable them to dart across fields and meadows with remarkable agility. European hares are primarily nocturnal animals, feeding on grasses, herbs, and crops under the cover of darkness.

In addition to hares, the Netherlands is also home to a diverse array of bird species, including waterfowl, raptors, and songbirds. The Wadden Sea, a UNESCO World Heritage Site located along the northern coast, is a vital habitat for migratory birds such as geese, ducks, and waders, which rely on its mudflats and marshes as a resting and feeding ground during their long journeys.

The Dutch coastline is teeming with life, with seals being a common sight along the sandy beaches and rocky shores. Harbor seals and gray seals can often be spotted basking in the sun or swimming in the shallow waters, especially in protected areas such as the Wadden Islands and the Oosterschelde National Park.

In the freshwater habitats of the Netherlands, a variety of fish species can be found, including pike, perch, and eel. The country's extensive network of rivers, lakes, and canals provides important spawning grounds and migration routes for these aquatic creatures, supporting both commercial and recreational fishing activities.

The Dutch countryside is also home to a rich diversity of plant life, with forests, wetlands, and meadows supporting a wide range of flora species. Common species include oak, beech, and birch trees in the forests, as well as reeds, sedges, and water lilies in the wetlands and marshes. The Keukenhof Gardens, located near the town of Lisse, are famous for their colorful displays of tulips, daffodils, and hyacinths, attracting visitors from around the world during the spring season.

In recent years, efforts have been made to restore and protect natural habitats in the Netherlands, including the creation of new nature reserves and the implementation of conservation programs for endangered species. These initiatives aim to safeguard the country's biodiversity and ensure that future generations can continue to enjoy the beauty and wonder of Dutch wildlife.

Tulips and Windmills: Symbols of Dutch Heritage

Tulips and windmills are two iconic symbols of Dutch heritage, deeply intertwined with the country's history, culture, and identity. These quintessentially Dutch symbols evoke images of colorful fields stretching as far as the eye can see, and majestic windmills standing tall against the horizon.

Tulips, with their vibrant hues and delicate petals, have been associated with the Netherlands for centuries. The Dutch tulip industry dates back to the 17th century when tulip bulbs became highly coveted commodities, fueling a speculative frenzy known as Tulip Mania. During this period, tulip bulbs were traded at exorbitant prices, making them a symbol of wealth and status.

Today, the Netherlands is the world's largest producer and exporter of tulips, with millions of bulbs cultivated each year for domestic and international markets. Tulip cultivation is concentrated in the western part of the country, particularly in the provinces of North Holland, South Holland, and Flevoland, where the cool climate and fertile soil provide ideal growing conditions.

The tulip season typically begins in late March and continues through May, with fields bursting into bloom in a riot of colors, including vibrant shades of red, yellow, pink, and purple. Visitors from around the world flock to the Netherlands during this time to witness the breathtaking spectacle of tulip fields in full bloom and to participate in events such as the Keukenhof Flower Exhibition, one of the largest flower gardens in the world.

Windmills are another enduring symbol of Dutch heritage, serving as both functional structures and cultural landmarks. Historically, windmills played a crucial role in harnessing wind power to pump water, grind grain, and saw timber, helping to drain the low-lying landscapes of the Netherlands and reclaim land from the sea.

While modern technology has largely supplanted traditional windmills for industrial purposes, many historic windmills still dot the Dutch countryside, serving as reminders of the country's ingenuity and resilience in the face of natural challenges. These picturesque structures, with their towering sails and distinctive silhouettes, are beloved symbols of Dutch culture and craftsmanship.

The Kinderdijk windmill complex, located near Rotterdam, is a UNESCO World Heritage Site and one of the most iconic windmill landscapes in the Netherlands. Dating back to the 18th century, the Kinderdijk windmills were built to control water levels in the surrounding polders, showcasing the innovative engineering skills of the Dutch people.

In addition to their practical functions, windmills have also inspired artists, writers, and poets throughout history, becoming enduring symbols of Dutch identity and pride. From Vincent van Gogh's famous paintings of windmills to Hans Brinker's fictional tale of the boy who saved his homeland by plugging a leaking dike with his finger, windmills have captured the imagination of people around the world.

In summary, tulips and windmills are not just symbols of Dutch heritage—they are living expressions of the country's history, culture, and ingenuity. Together, they embody the spirit of the Netherlands, a nation that has embraced its natural surroundings and transformed them into enduring symbols of beauty, strength, and resilience.

Cycling Culture: Pedaling Through the Netherlands

Cycling culture runs deep in the Netherlands, where bicycles are not just a mode of transportation but a way of life. From bustling city streets to serene countryside paths, cycling is an integral part of Dutch culture, shaping the daily routines and lifestyles of millions of people.

The Netherlands is renowned as one of the most bike-friendly countries in the world, with a comprehensive network of cycling infrastructure that includes dedicated bike lanes, traffic signals, and parking facilities. Cyclists enjoy priority on many roads, and cities are designed with biking in mind, making it safe and convenient to travel by bike.

Dutch cities, such as Amsterdam and Utrecht, are famous for their bike-friendly streets and bustling cycling scenes. Bicycles outnumber cars in many urban areas, and cycling is often the fastest and most efficient way to get around. Bike-sharing programs and rental services make it easy for residents and visitors alike to explore the city on two wheels.

Cycling is not just a practical mode of transportation in the Netherlands—it's also a cherished recreational activity and a popular pastime for people of all ages. Families, friends, and couples often take leisurely bike rides through scenic parks, along picturesque canals, and across expansive polders, enjoying the fresh air and beautiful landscapes.

One of the highlights of Dutch cycling culture is the annual bicycle race known as the Elfstedentocht, or Eleven Cities Tour. Held in the province of Friesland, this long-distance cycling event takes participants on a 200-kilometer journey through eleven historic cities, challenging riders to test their endurance and skill on the flat, windswept terrain.

Cycling plays a significant role in promoting health and wellness in the Netherlands, with many people incorporating biking into their daily routines as a form of exercise and stress relief. Commuting by bike is not only good for the environment but also beneficial for physical and mental well-being, helping to reduce traffic congestion and air pollution while improving cardiovascular fitness and overall quality of life.

The Dutch government has long recognized the importance of cycling as a sustainable and healthy mode of transportation, investing heavily in infrastructure and initiatives to promote cycling culture. The Netherlands has set ambitious targets to increase the share of trips made by bike, with the goal of becoming carbon-neutral and car-free in the future.

In recent years, cycling has gained popularity as a global trend, with cities around the world adopting Dutch-inspired bike-friendly policies and infrastructure. The Dutch approach to cycling, with its emphasis on safety, accessibility, and inclusivity, serves as a model for sustainable urban planning and transportation design worldwide.

In conclusion, cycling culture is deeply ingrained in the fabric of Dutch society, reflecting the country's commitment to sustainability, health, and community. Whether commuting to work, running errands, or enjoying a leisurely ride, cycling is a way of life in the Netherlands—a testament to the enduring power of pedal power in shaping our cities and our lives.

Dutch Festivals and Traditions: Celebrating Life

Dutch festivals and traditions are vibrant celebrations that bring communities together to honor their heritage, express creativity, and revel in the joy of life. From centuries-old traditions rooted in religious and cultural practices to modern events that showcase Dutch innovation and diversity, the Netherlands boasts a rich tapestry of festivities that captivate locals and visitors alike.

One of the most famous Dutch festivals is King's Day, or Koningsdag, celebrated on April 27th each year in honor of the King's birthday. This national holiday is marked by lively street parties, flea markets, and concerts across the country, with people dressed in orange—the national color—taking to the streets to celebrate with music, dancing, and merriment.

Another beloved tradition in the Netherlands is Sinterklaas, a festive celebration held on December 5th to honor Saint Nicholas, the patron saint of children. Sinterklaas arrives in the Netherlands from Spain by steamboat, accompanied by his helpers, known as Zwarte Piet or Black Pete. Children leave out their shoes on the night of December 5th, hoping to find them filled with presents and treats the next morning.

Carnival, known as Carnaval, is a colorful and exuberant festival celebrated in the southern provinces of the Netherlands, particularly in Limburg and North Brabant. The festivities typically take place in February or March and feature parades, costume parties, and street performances, with revelers donning elaborate masks and costumes to join in the fun.

The Netherlands is also known for its vibrant music festivals, which attract thousands of music fans from around the world. Events such as Pinkpop, Lowlands, and North Sea Jazz Festival showcase a diverse lineup of musical genres, including rock, pop, jazz, and electronic music, with performances by both international superstars and up-and-coming artists.

For those with a taste for the theatrical, the Netherlands hosts a variety of cultural festivals that celebrate the performing arts in all their forms. The Holland Festival, held annually in Amsterdam, showcases cutting-edge theater, dance, and music performances from around the world, while the

International Film Festival Rotterdam highlights innovative and boundary-pushing cinema.

Religious traditions also play a significant role in Dutch culture, with holidays such as Easter and Christmas celebrated with religious services, family gatherings, and festive meals. In addition, many Dutch towns and villages hold annual processions, parades, and reenactments to commemorate religious events and historical milestones.

Throughout the year, Dutch communities come together to celebrate local traditions and customs that are unique to their region. From cheese markets in Alkmaar to flower parades in Bloemencorso, each town and city in the Netherlands has its own distinct festivals and rituals that reflect its cultural heritage and identity.

In summary, Dutch festivals and traditions are vibrant expressions of the country's rich cultural heritage and diverse communities. Whether celebrating a royal birthday, honoring a beloved saint, or reveling in the joys of music and art, the Netherlands offers a wealth of opportunities to experience the magic of life through its festive celebrations and cherished traditions.

Dutch Art and Architecture: Rembrandt to Van Gogh

Dutch art and architecture have long been celebrated for their innovation, creativity, and influence on the world stage. From the masterpieces of the Dutch Golden Age to the avant-garde movements of the 20th century, the Netherlands has produced a wealth of artistic talent that continues to captivate audiences around the globe.

The Dutch Golden Age, spanning the 17th century, was a period of unprecedented prosperity and cultural flourishing in the Netherlands. It was during this time that Dutch artists such as Rembrandt van Rijn, Johannes Vermeer, and Frans Hals produced some of their most iconic works, including masterpieces like "The Night Watch," "Girl with a Pearl Earring," and "The Laughing Cavalier."

Rembrandt van Rijn, often regarded as one of the greatest painters in the history of Western art, was known for his mastery of light and shadow, as well as his ability to capture the complexities of human emotion. His paintings, drawings, and etchings are celebrated for their dramatic intensity and profound psychological insight, making him a towering figure in Dutch art history.

Johannes Vermeer, another luminary of the Dutch Golden Age, was celebrated for his exquisite use of light and color, as well as his meticulous attention to detail. His paintings, which often depicted scenes of domestic life and everyday moments, are characterized by their luminous beauty and timeless appeal, earning him a reputation as a master of the genre known as genre painting.

In addition to painting, Dutch artists of the Golden Age also made significant contributions to the fields of printmaking, sculpture, and decorative arts. The works of artists such as Hendrick Avercamp, Pieter Bruegel the Elder, and Jan Steen are prized for their technical skill, imaginative vision, and keen observations of Dutch society and culture.

Dutch architecture is equally renowned for its ingenuity, with iconic landmarks such as the Rijksmuseum, Amsterdam's Central Station, and the Van Nelle Factory showcasing the country's rich architectural heritage. The traditional Dutch architectural style, characterized by its use of brick, gables, and stepped facades, is exemplified in historic buildings such as canal houses, windmills, and churches.

In the 20th century, Dutch art and architecture witnessed a period of experimentation and innovation, with movements such as De Stijl, Bauhaus, and Dutch modernism leaving an indelible mark on the cultural landscape. Artists such as Piet Mondrian, Gerrit Rietveld, and Willem de Kooning embraced abstraction, minimalism, and geometric forms, pushing the boundaries of traditional artistic conventions.

Today, Dutch art and architecture continue to thrive, with contemporary artists and architects exploring new ideas, materials, and technologies to create works that challenge, inspire, and provoke thought. Whether wandering through the galleries of world-class museums, exploring the streets of historic cities, or marveling at cutting-edge architectural designs, visitors to the Netherlands are sure to be captivated by the rich tapestry of artistic expression that defines this vibrant and dynamic country.

Dutch Music: From Classical to Electronic

Dutch music is a diverse and dynamic tapestry that reflects the country's rich cultural heritage and innovative spirit. From classical compositions to cutting-edge electronic beats, the Netherlands has made significant contributions to the global music scene, producing world-renowned artists and pioneering new genres along the way.

Classical music has a long tradition in the Netherlands, with composers such as Jan Pieterszoon Sweelinck and Willem Pijper leaving lasting legacies in the world of classical composition. Sweelinck, known as the "Orpheus of Amsterdam," was a renowned organist and composer who helped establish the Dutch organ school, while Pijper was a leading figure in the modernist movement, pushing the boundaries of traditional musical forms.

In the 17th and 18th centuries, Dutch composers made significant contributions to the development of baroque music, with figures such as Jacob van Eyck and Johan Wagenaar producing notable works for organ, choir, and chamber ensemble. The music of the Dutch Golden Age reflected the country's growing prosperity and cultural sophistication, with composers drawing inspiration from the rich tapestry of Dutch life and landscape.

The 19th century saw a resurgence of interest in Dutch folk music, with composers such as Johannes Verhulst and Julius Röntgen incorporating folk melodies and themes into their compositions. This period also witnessed the rise of the Dutch symphony orchestra, with the formation of institutions such as the Royal Concertgebouw Orchestra, one of the leading orchestras in the world.

In the 20th century, Dutch music experienced a period of experimentation and innovation, with artists exploring new genres and pushing the boundaries of traditional musical forms. The emergence of jazz, blues, and rock 'n' roll influenced Dutch musicians, leading to the development of unique hybrid styles such as Nederpop and Dutch rock.

The Netherlands has also been a pioneer in the electronic music scene, with artists such as Tiësto, Armin van Buuren, and Afrojack achieving international acclaim for their innovative productions and electrifying performances. Dutch DJs and producers have played a leading role in shaping the global electronic music landscape, with Amsterdam's dance music scene earning a reputation as one of the most vibrant and influential in the world.

In addition to electronic music, the Netherlands has a thriving pop and indie music scene, with bands such as Golden Earring, Shocking Blue, and Kensington achieving success both at home and abroad. Dutch pop music often incorporates elements of rock, folk, and electronic music, resulting in a diverse and eclectic sound that resonates with audiences around the world.

Today, Dutch music continues to evolve and innovate, with artists exploring new genres, technologies, and creative possibilities. Whether performing in concert halls, clubs, or festivals, Dutch musicians are celebrated for their talent, creativity, and passion for music, making the Netherlands a vibrant and dynamic hub of musical innovation and expression.

Dutch Literature: From Erasmus to Harry Mulisch

Dutch literature is a rich tapestry woven with the threads of history, culture, and imagination, spanning centuries of creative expression and intellectual exploration. From the works of Erasmus, the Renaissance humanist and scholar, to modern-day authors like Harry Mulisch, Dutch literature has made significant contributions to the world of letters, inspiring readers with its depth, diversity, and enduring relevance.

Erasmus, born in Rotterdam in 1466, is best known for his influential works on philosophy, theology, and education. His most famous work, "In Praise of Folly," is a satirical critique of the follies and vices of society, written in a witty and engaging style that continues to resonate with readers today. Erasmus's emphasis on reason, tolerance, and humanism laid the groundwork for the Dutch Enlightenment and the flowering of intellectual thought in the Netherlands.

In the 17th century, the Dutch Golden Age witnessed a flourishing of literature, with writers such as Joost van den Vondel, Constantijn Huygens, and Pieter Corneliszoon Hooft producing works of poetry, drama, and prose that reflected the cultural and intellectual ferment of the time. Vondel, known as the "Prince of Dutch Poets," wrote epic poems, tragedies, and historical plays that explored themes of morality, religion, and national identity.

The 19th century saw the rise of romanticism in Dutch literature, with writers such as Eduard Douwes Dekker (Multatuli) and Louis Couperus exploring themes of love, nature, and individualism in their novels and essays. Multatuli's novel "Max Havelaar," a scathing indictment of colonial exploitation in the Dutch East Indies, sparked a national debate on ethics and social justice, inspiring reform movements and political activism.

In the 20th century, Dutch literature underwent a period of experimentation and innovation, with writers exploring new forms, styles, and themes in response to the tumultuous events of the time. Authors such as Nescio, Simon Vestdijk, and Gerard Reve experimented with stream-of-consciousness narration, surrealism, and existentialism, pushing the boundaries of traditional literary conventions and challenging readers to reconsider their assumptions about reality and identity.

One of the most celebrated figures in modern Dutch literature is Harry Mulisch, whose novels, including "The Assault" and "The Discovery of Heaven," have earned him international acclaim and literary awards. Mulisch's works explore themes of history, memory, and destiny, weaving together elements of philosophy, science, and mythology to create richly layered narratives that resonate with readers across cultures and generations.

In addition to novelists, Dutch literature is also home to a diverse array of poets, playwrights, and essayists who continue to enrich the literary landscape with their distinctive voices and perspectives. From the lyrical poetry of Gerrit Achterberg to the experimental theater of Hugo Claus, Dutch writers have embraced a spirit of innovation and creativity that reflects the dynamism and diversity of Dutch culture.

Today, Dutch literature remains a vibrant and thriving tradition, with contemporary authors such as Arnon Grunberg, Connie Palmen, and Herman Koch carrying on the legacy of their predecessors and exploring new directions in storytelling and expression. Whether exploring the complexities of human nature, grappling with existential questions, or simply delighting readers with tales of adventure and imagination, Dutch literature continues to captivate and inspire audiences around the world.

Dutch Education System: Excellence and Inclusivity

The Dutch education system is renowned for its commitment to excellence and inclusivity, providing students with a high-quality education that prepares them for success in an increasingly globalized world. From early childhood education to higher education, the Netherlands offers a comprehensive and accessible system that prioritizes academic rigor, critical thinking, and personal development.

One of the hallmarks of the Dutch education system is its emphasis on inclusivity and equal opportunity for all students, regardless of background or ability. Education is compulsory for children between the ages of 5 and 16, and the government provides funding to ensure that all children have access to free, high-quality education.

The Dutch education system is divided into several stages, beginning with primary education, which typically lasts for eight years. Primary schools in the Netherlands focus on developing foundational skills in reading, writing, and mathematics, as well as fostering creativity, curiosity, and social skills.

After primary school, students move on to secondary education, which is divided into several tracks based on academic ability and career aspirations. The most common track is the VMBO (preparatory secondary vocational education), which prepares students for vocational training or entry-level employment. Other tracks include HAVO (higher general continued education) and VWO (pre-university education), which provide a more academic curriculum and prepare students for higher education.

In addition to traditional academic subjects, the Dutch education system also places a strong emphasis on practical skills and vocational training. Vocational education and training (VET) programs are available for students who prefer hands-on learning and are interested in pursuing careers in fields such as healthcare, technology, and hospitality.

Higher education in the Netherlands is characterized by its diversity and international orientation, with a wide range of programs offered in English to attract students from around the world. Dutch universities are known for their high academic standards, cutting-edge research facilities, and strong emphasis on innovation and entrepreneurship.

The Dutch government invests heavily in education, allocating a significant portion of its budget to support schools, universities, and research institutions. In addition to public funding, the Netherlands has a thriving private education sector, with a growing number of international schools and private universities offering alternative educational options.

The Dutch education system is also known for its innovative pedagogical approaches and commitment to continuous improvement. Teachers are highly trained and respected professionals, and schools have autonomy to develop their own curriculum and teaching methods based on the needs of their students.

Overall, the Dutch education system is a testament to the country's commitment to excellence, equity, and innovation in education. By providing students with a solid foundation of knowledge, skills, and values, the Netherlands prepares future generations to thrive in a rapidly changing world and contribute to the global community.

Dutch Healthcare: A Model of Efficiency

Dutch healthcare is often lauded as a model of efficiency, combining universal coverage with high-quality care and cost-effective delivery. The Netherlands has a decentralized healthcare system that emphasizes competition, choice, and patient-centered care, making it one of the most advanced healthcare systems in the world.

One of the key features of the Dutch healthcare system is its emphasis on universal coverage, with all residents required to have health insurance. The system is based on a combination of public and private insurance, with individuals required to purchase basic health insurance from private insurers, supplemented by additional coverage for dental care, physiotherapy, and other services.

The Dutch government plays a regulatory role in the healthcare system, setting standards for quality, safety, and affordability, while private insurers compete for customers based on price, service, and coverage options. This competitive marketplace encourages innovation and efficiency, driving improvements in care delivery and patient outcomes.

Primary care is the foundation of the Dutch healthcare system, with general practitioners serving as the first point of contact for most patients. General practitioners provide a wide range of services, including preventive care, diagnosis, treatment, and referrals to specialists or hospitals when needed. Patients have the freedom to choose their own general practitioner, and most practices offer same-day appointments and extended hours to accommodate busy schedules.

In addition to primary care, the Dutch healthcare system provides access to a comprehensive range of specialist services, including hospitals, mental health care, maternity care, and long-term care. Hospitals in the Netherlands are known for their high-quality care and state-of-the-art facilities, with many offering specialized services such as cancer treatment, organ transplants, and robotic surgery.

The Dutch healthcare system also places a strong emphasis on preventive care and public health initiatives, with programs aimed at promoting healthy lifestyles, preventing chronic diseases, and reducing healthcare disparities. The government invests in initiatives to address social determinants of health, such as poverty, education, and housing, recognizing that these factors play a significant role in determining health outcomes.

Despite its many strengths, the Dutch healthcare system faces challenges, including rising healthcare costs, an aging population, and increasing demand for services. To address these challenges, the government is implementing reforms aimed at improving efficiency, reducing waste, and promoting value-based care. Initiatives such as bundled payments, integrated care models, and electronic health records are being rolled out to streamline care delivery and improve coordination among providers.

Overall, the Dutch healthcare system is a testament to the country's commitment to universal coverage, patient-centered care, and innovation in healthcare delivery. By combining elements of public and private insurance with a focus on competition, choice, and quality, the Netherlands has created a healthcare system that delivers excellent care to its residents while controlling costs and promoting efficiency.

Dutch Innovation: Driving Global Progress

Dutch innovation has long been recognized as a driving force behind global progress, with the Netherlands consistently ranking among the world's most innovative countries. From groundbreaking discoveries in science and technology to cutting-edge solutions in sustainability and design, Dutch innovators have made significant contributions to a wide range of fields, shaping the future of industries and improving lives around the world.

One of the key factors driving Dutch innovation is the country's strong tradition of collaboration between government, academia, and industry. Public-private partnerships are common in the Netherlands, with government funding and support provided to research institutions, startups, and established companies to develop new products, processes, and technologies. This collaborative approach fosters creativity, encourages knowledge sharing, and accelerates the pace of innovation.

The Netherlands is home to a vibrant ecosystem of research institutions, universities, and tech hubs that serve as catalysts for innovation. Institutions such as Delft University of Technology, Wageningen University & Research, and Eindhoven University of Technology are renowned for their world-class research facilities and interdisciplinary approach to problem-solving. These institutions collaborate closely with industry partners to translate research findings into real-world applications and drive technological advancement.

In addition to academic research, the Netherlands is a hotbed of entrepreneurial activity, with a thriving startup ecosystem that supports innovation and entrepreneurship. Cities such as Amsterdam, Rotterdam, and Eindhoven are hubs for startups and scale-ups, offering access to funding, mentorship, and networking opportunities for aspiring entrepreneurs. The Dutch government provides support for startups through initiatives such as tax incentives, grants, and incubator programs, helping to foster a culture of innovation and risk-taking.

The Netherlands is also at the forefront of innovation in sustainability and renewable energy, with a strong commitment to combating climate change and promoting environmental stewardship. Dutch companies and research institutions are leading the way in developing clean energy technologies such as wind power, solar energy, and biofuels, as well as innovative solutions for waste management, water conservation, and urban planning. The Dutch government has set ambitious targets for reducing carbon emissions and transitioning to a circular economy, driving investment and innovation in green technologies and sustainable practices.

In the field of healthcare and life sciences, Dutch innovation is revolutionizing the way we diagnose, treat, and prevent disease. The Netherlands is home to world-class hospitals, research institutes, and pharmaceutical companies that are pioneering new therapies, medical devices, and diagnostic tools. From groundbreaking discoveries in genomics and personalized medicine to advances in digital health and telemedicine, Dutch innovators are harnessing the power of technology and data to improve healthcare outcomes and enhance patient care.

Dutch innovation extends beyond traditional sectors to include creative industries such as design, fashion, and architecture. Dutch designers and artists are celebrated for their bold ideas, unconventional approaches, and commitment to sustainability and social responsibility. Design innovations such as the Dutch Design Week in Eindhoven showcase the latest trends and breakthroughs in design, while Dutch fashion designers such as Viktor & Rolf and Iris van Herpen are renowned for their avant-garde creations and experimental techniques.

In summary, Dutch innovation is a driving force behind global progress, with the Netherlands at the forefront of technological advancement, sustainability, healthcare innovation, and creative expression. Through collaboration, entrepreneurship, and a commitment to excellence, Dutch innovators are shaping the future and making the world a better place for generations to come.

Religious Diversity in the Netherlands

Religious diversity in the Netherlands reflects a rich tapestry of beliefs and traditions that have evolved over centuries, shaped by waves of immigration, cultural exchange, and social change. The Netherlands is known for its tolerance and openness to different religious practices, making it a welcoming home to people of various faiths from around the world.

Historically, the Netherlands has been predominantly Christian, with Roman Catholicism and Protestantism being the two major branches of Christianity practiced in the country. Catholicism has deep roots in Dutch history, dating back to the Middle Ages when the Netherlands was part of the Holy Roman Empire. Protestantism gained prominence during the Reformation in the 16th century, leading to the establishment of the Dutch Reformed Church and other Protestant denominations.

In addition to Christianity, the Netherlands is home to a significant Muslim population, primarily consisting of immigrants from Turkey, Morocco, Suriname, and Indonesia. Islam is the second-largest religion in the Netherlands, with mosques and Islamic centers serving as places of worship and community gathering for Muslim communities across the country. The practice of Islam in the Netherlands is diverse, with Sunni, Shiite, and Sufi traditions represented among the Muslim population.

Judaism also has a long history in the Netherlands, dating back to the Middle Ages when Jewish communities settled in cities such as Amsterdam, Rotterdam, and The Hague. Despite facing periods of persecution and discrimination, Dutch Jews have made significant contributions to Dutch society and culture, particularly in the fields of commerce, finance, and the arts. Today, the Jewish community in the Netherlands remains vibrant, with synagogues, schools, and cultural institutions preserving and celebrating Jewish heritage and traditions.

In addition to Christianity, Islam, and Judaism, the Netherlands is home to smaller religious communities, including Hinduism, Buddhism, and Sikhism. These faiths have been brought to the Netherlands by immigrants from South Asia, Southeast Asia, and other parts of the world, contributing to the country's religious diversity and cultural tapestry.

The Dutch government is committed to upholding religious freedom and protecting the rights of individuals to practice their faith without discrimination. The Netherlands has a secular government that is separate from religious institutions, ensuring that all citizens have equal rights and opportunities regardless of their religious beliefs or affiliations.

Interfaith dialogue and cooperation are encouraged in the Netherlands, with religious organizations and community groups working together to promote understanding, tolerance, and social cohesion. Events such as interfaith prayer services, cultural festivals, and community outreach programs provide opportunities for people of different faiths to come together, learn from one another, and build bridges of friendship and solidarity.

Despite its tradition of religious tolerance, the Netherlands has also grappled with issues of religious extremism and radicalization, particularly in the wake of global terrorist attacks and geopolitical conflicts. The Dutch government has implemented measures to prevent radicalization and promote social integration, including efforts to engage with religious communities, address socio-economic disparities, and promote democratic values and human rights.

Overall, religious diversity in the Netherlands is a source of strength and resilience, reflecting the country's commitment to pluralism, tolerance, and freedom of belief. By embracing and celebrating its diverse religious heritage, the Netherlands continues to enrich its cultural landscape and foster a spirit of inclusivity and respect for all.

Dutch Tolerance: Acceptance and Openness

Dutch tolerance is a cornerstone of Dutch society, rooted in a long history of cultural exchange, liberalism, and respect for individual freedoms. The Netherlands is renowned for its progressive attitudes toward diversity, acceptance, and openness, making it one of the most tolerant countries in the world.

The concept of Dutch tolerance dates back centuries, with the Dutch Republic in the 17th century known for its religious and cultural pluralism. During this period, the Netherlands became a refuge for religious minorities fleeing persecution in other parts of Europe, including Jews, Protestants, and Catholics. The Dutch Republic adopted a policy of religious tolerance, allowing different faiths to coexist peacefully and practice their beliefs without fear of discrimination or persecution.

In addition to religious tolerance, the Netherlands has a long tradition of social tolerance, with a liberal approach to issues such as drug policy, LGBTQ+ rights, and euthanasia. The Dutch government has implemented progressive policies to promote equality, protect human rights, and ensure the rights and dignity of all citizens, regardless of their background or identity.

The Netherlands was one of the first countries in the world to legalize same-sex marriage in 2001, reflecting its commitment to LGBTQ+ rights and equality under the law. The country has since adopted a range of measures to combat discrimination and promote inclusivity, including anti-discrimination laws, hate crime legislation, and public awareness campaigns.

The Dutch approach to drug policy is characterized by pragmatism and harm reduction, with a focus on public health and safety rather than punitive measures. The Netherlands decriminalized the possession and use of small quantities of cannabis in the 1970s, leading to the establishment of regulated cannabis cafes (known as "coffee shops") where adults can purchase and consume cannabis in a controlled environment. While the sale and production of cannabis remain illegal, the Dutch government tolerates the existence of coffee shops as part of its harm reduction strategy.

In the field of healthcare, the Netherlands is known for its progressive approach to end-of-life care and euthanasia. Euthanasia and physician-assisted suicide have been legal in the Netherlands since 2002 under strict conditions, allowing terminally ill patients to request medical assistance to end their lives in a humane and dignified manner. The Dutch government regulates euthanasia through a system of checks and balances to ensure that it is carried out in accordance with legal and ethical guidelines.

Despite its reputation for tolerance, the Netherlands has also faced challenges and controversies related to issues such as immigration, multiculturalism, and social cohesion. In recent years, debates over integration, identity, and national values have fueled tensions and divisions within Dutch society, prompting reflection and debate about the meaning and limits of Dutch tolerance in a rapidly changing world.

Overall, Dutch tolerance is a defining characteristic of Dutch culture and identity, reflecting a commitment to openness, diversity, and respect for individual freedoms. By embracing and celebrating its multicultural heritage, the Netherlands continues to strive towards a more inclusive and equitable society where all people can live and thrive in harmony.

Dutch Sense of Humor: Wit and Sarcasm

The Dutch sense of humor is often characterized by its wit, irony, and sarcasm, reflecting a dry and understated style that can sometimes be misunderstood by those unfamiliar with Dutch culture. While humor is subjective and varies from person to person, there are certain elements that are commonly associated with Dutch humor, rooted in the country's history, culture, and social norms.

One aspect of Dutch humor is its reliance on irony and self-deprecation, with many Dutch people embracing a modest and down-to-earth attitude that eschews arrogance or pretension. This self-deprecating humor can be seen in everyday interactions, where people may poke fun at themselves or their own foibles as a way of connecting with others and diffusing tension.

Sarcasm is another hallmark of Dutch humor, with many Dutch people using dry wit and sarcasm as a form of communication and social interaction. Sarcasm is often employed as a means of expressing dissatisfaction or skepticism, with Dutch people using humor to critique social norms, authority figures, or prevailing attitudes.

Dutch humor also tends to be direct and straightforward, with little tolerance for pretense or artifice. This directness can sometimes come across as blunt or insensitive to those from cultures that place a greater emphasis on politeness and diplomacy. However, in Dutch culture, honesty and authenticity are valued, and humor is often used as a way of cutting through social niceties and getting to the heart of a matter.

One of the most famous examples of Dutch humor is the tradition of "Dutch stand-up comedy," which has gained popularity in recent years with comedians such as Theo Maassen, Ronald Goedemondt, and Claudia de Breij gaining international acclaim for their sharp wit and observational humor. Dutch stand-up comedy often tackles taboo subjects with honesty and candor, challenging audiences to confront uncomfortable truths while still finding humor in the absurdity of everyday life.

In addition to stand-up comedy, Dutch humor is also evident in the country's rich tradition of satire and political commentary. Satirical television programs such as "Zondag met Lubach" and "Dit was het nieuws" use humor to critique politicians, media figures, and societal trends, providing a platform for critical thinking and social commentary in a lighthearted and entertaining manner.

While Dutch humor may not always be to everyone's taste, it plays an important role in Dutch culture, serving as a means of bonding, coping with adversity, and challenging the status quo. Whether it's through dry wit, sarcasm, or self-deprecation, the Dutch have a unique and distinctive approach to humor that reflects their values, attitudes, and outlook on life.

Dutch Sports: From Football to Ice Skating

Dutch sports culture is vibrant and diverse, with a rich history of athletic achievement across a wide range of disciplines. One of the most popular sports in the Netherlands is football, which enjoys widespread participation and passionate fan support. Dutch football clubs such as Ajax Amsterdam, PSV Eindhoven, and Feyenoord Rotterdam have achieved success both domestically and internationally, with Ajax particularly renowned for its youth development program and attractive playing style.

In addition to football, the Netherlands is also known for its prowess in speed skating, with Dutch athletes consistently performing well in international competitions such as the Winter Olympics and World Championships. The Dutch have a strong tradition of speed skating, dating back centuries to when frozen canals and waterways provided a natural setting for the sport. Today, Dutch speed skaters dominate the sport, with athletes such as Sven Kramer, Ireen Wüst, and Jorien ter Mors among the most decorated in history.

Cycling is another popular sport in the Netherlands, with the country's flat terrain and extensive network of bike paths making it ideal for recreational and competitive cycling. Dutch cyclists excel in road racing, track cycling, and BMX, with the Netherlands boasting a strong cycling culture and numerous world-class riders. The annual Tour de France often features Dutch riders competing for stage wins and overall classification honors.

Field hockey is also widely played and highly regarded in the Netherlands, with both the men's and women's national teams consistently ranked among the best in the world. Dutch field hockey teams have won numerous Olympic medals and World Cup titles, with the women's team in particular enjoying sustained success at the highest level.

In addition to these traditional sports, the Netherlands has also produced world-class athletes in sports such as gymnastics, judo, volleyball, and rowing. Dutch athletes have excelled on the international stage in a variety of disciplines, showcasing the country's depth and versatility in sports.

The Dutch government and sports organizations are committed to promoting physical activity and sports participation at all levels, with initiatives aimed at encouraging youth involvement, supporting elite athletes, and investing in sports infrastructure and facilities. The Netherlands also hosts major sporting events such as the UEFA European Championship, the Tour de France, and the ISU Speed Skating World Cup, attracting athletes and spectators from around the world.

Overall, Dutch sports culture is characterized by a passion for competition, a commitment to excellence, and a sense of pride in representing the Netherlands on the global stage. Whether it's on the football pitch, the ice rink, or the cycling track, Dutch athletes continue to inspire and captivate audiences with their talent, determination, and sportsmanship.

Dutch Design: Sleek, Functional, Iconic

Dutch design is celebrated worldwide for its sleek, functional, and iconic aesthetics that have left an indelible mark on the world of art, architecture, fashion, and product design. Rooted in a tradition of innovation, craftsmanship, and pragmatism, Dutch design reflects the country's unique cultural heritage and its commitment to creativity and ingenuity.

One of the defining characteristics of Dutch design is its emphasis on functionality and practicality. Dutch designers are known for their minimalist approach, focusing on clean lines, geometric shapes, and efficient use of space. Whether it's furniture, household appliances, or urban infrastructure, Dutch design prioritizes usability and user experience, ensuring that products are not only visually appealing but also highly functional and user-friendly.

Another hallmark of Dutch design is its commitment to sustainability and environmental stewardship. Dutch designers are at the forefront of the green design movement, incorporating sustainable materials, energy-efficient technologies, and eco-friendly production methods into their work. From eco-friendly furniture made from recycled materials to energy-efficient buildings with green roofs and solar panels, Dutch design is leading the way in creating a more sustainable and environmentally conscious world. Dutch design is also known for its iconic contributions to the world of architecture, with architects such as Rem Koolhaas, MVRDV, and UNStudio gaining international acclaim for their innovative and visionary designs. From the futuristic skyline of Rotterdam to the historic canals of Amsterdam, Dutch architects have transformed the urban landscape with bold, cutting-edge designs that push the boundaries of what is possible in architecture.

In the realm of fashion, Dutch designers are celebrated for their avant-garde creations and experimental techniques. Designers such as Viktor & Rolf, Iris van Herpen, and Bas Kosters have gained recognition for their bold and imaginative designs, blending traditional craftsmanship with cutting-edge technology to create wearable works of art. Dutch fashion is known for its edgy, contemporary aesthetic and its ability to challenge conventions and push the boundaries of fashion.

Dutch design has also made significant contributions to the world of graphic design, typography, and visual communication. Dutch graphic designers such as Wim Crouwel, Irma Boom, and Experimental Jetset are renowned for their innovative use of typography, color, and layout, creating visually stunning designs that communicate complex ideas and emotions with clarity and precision.

In summary, Dutch design is a testament to the country's rich cultural heritage, spirit of innovation, and commitment to excellence. Whether it's in the realm of architecture, fashion, product design, or graphic design, Dutch designers continue to push the boundaries of creativity and imagination, leaving an enduring legacy that inspires and captivates audiences around the world.

Dutch Technology and Engineering: Leading the Way

Dutch technology and engineering have long been at the forefront of innovation and progress, with the Netherlands playing a significant role in shaping the modern world through its contributions to various fields. From pioneering advancements in water management and maritime engineering to breakthroughs in renewable energy and high-tech industries, Dutch expertise and ingenuity continue to drive global progress and development.

One of the most notable areas of Dutch technology is water management and hydraulic engineering. Situated below sea level, much of the Netherlands is vulnerable to flooding, making effective water management crucial for the country's survival. Over the centuries, the Dutch have developed an extensive system of dikes, dams, and canals to control water levels and prevent flooding. Projects such as the Delta Works, a series of dams and storm surge barriers built to protect the Dutch coastline, are considered marvels of engineering and have inspired similar projects around the world. In addition to water management, the Netherlands is also a leader in maritime engineering and port infrastructure. Rotterdam, Europe's largest port, is a hub of maritime activity and a vital link in global trade networks. Dutch engineers have developed innovative solutions for container handling, shipbuilding, and logistics, making Rotterdam one of the most efficient and technologically advanced ports in the world. Renewable energy is another area where Dutch technology and engineering excel. The Netherlands is a pioneer in wind energy, with offshore wind farms generating a significant portion of the country's electricity. Dutch companies such as Royal Dutch Shell and Siemens Gamesa are leading the way in developing offshore wind turbines and technology, helping to reduce carbon emissions and combat climate change.

The Netherlands is also a hotspot for high-tech industries such as aerospace, biotechnology, and nanotechnology. Dutch companies and research institutions are at the forefront of innovation in fields such as space exploration, medical research, and semiconductor technology. Amsterdam's Science Park and Eindhoven's High Tech Campus are home to numerous tech startups, research labs, and multinational corporations, fostering collaboration and innovation in the tech sector.

Furthermore, the Dutch government and private sector are investing heavily in emerging technologies such as artificial intelligence, blockchain, and quantum computing. Initiatives such as the Dutch AI Coalition and the Dutch Blockchain Coalition bring together industry leaders, researchers, and policymakers to drive innovation and establish the Netherlands as a global leader in cutting-edge technologies.

In summary, Dutch technology and engineering are driving forces behind the country's economic prosperity and global influence. From water management and maritime engineering to renewable energy and high-tech industries, Dutch expertise and innovation continue to shape the world in profound ways, paving the way for a more sustainable, connected, and prosperous future.

Dutch Transport: Navigating the Lowlands

Dutch transport infrastructure is highly developed and efficient, catering to the needs of a densely populated country with a strategic location in Europe. With a network of roads, railways, waterways, and airports, the Netherlands offers a variety of options for navigating the lowlands.

Road transportation is a primary mode of travel in the Netherlands, with an extensive network of highways, expressways, and local roads connecting cities, towns, and rural areas. The Dutch road network is well-maintained and well-signposted, making it easy for motorists to navigate the country. Major highways such as the A1, A2, and A4 provide efficient connections between cities, while smaller roads crisscross the countryside, offering scenic routes through picturesque landscapes.

Public transportation is also popular in the Netherlands, with an extensive network of trains, buses, trams, and ferries serving urban and rural areas alike. The Nederlandse Spoorwegen (NS) operates the national railway system, with frequent and reliable train services connecting major cities and towns across the country. The Dutch rail network is known for its punctuality and efficiency, making train travel a convenient option for commuters and tourists alike.

In addition to trains, buses and trams provide convenient and affordable transportation options within cities and regions. Major cities such as Amsterdam, Rotterdam, and The Hague have extensive public transportation networks, including metro systems, tram lines, and bus routes, making it easy for residents and visitors to get around without a car. The OV-chipkaart, a smart card system, allows passengers to pay for public transportation seamlessly, making transfers between different modes of transport simple and efficient.

Water transportation has long been important in the Netherlands, given the country's extensive network of rivers, canals, and waterways. The Port of Rotterdam is the largest seaport in Europe and plays a crucial role in international trade, handling goods and cargo from around the world. In addition to maritime shipping, inland waterways such as the Rhine, Meuse, and Scheldt rivers are used for transporting goods and passengers within the country and to neighboring countries.

Cycling is also a popular mode of transportation in the Netherlands, with dedicated bike lanes and paths crisscrossing the country. Dutch cities are known for their bike-friendly infrastructure, with ample bike parking, bike-sharing programs, and priority given to cyclists at intersections. Many Dutch people use bicycles as their primary mode of transportation for commuting to work, running errands, and leisure activities, contributing to a healthier and more sustainable lifestyle.

Finally, air transportation is facilitated by several international airports in the Netherlands, including Amsterdam Airport Schiphol, Rotterdam The Hague Airport, and Eindhoven Airport. Amsterdam Airport Schiphol is one of the busiest airports in Europe and serves as a major hub for international flights, connecting the Netherlands to destinations around the world.

In summary, Dutch transport infrastructure is diverse, efficient, and well-integrated, offering a variety of options for navigating the lowlands. Whether by road, rail, water, bike, or air, travelers in the Netherlands enjoy convenient and reliable transportation options that cater to their needs and preferences.

Dutch Economy: Resilience and Prosperity

The Dutch economy is renowned for its resilience and prosperity, supported by a diverse range of industries, a highly skilled workforce, and a favorable business environment. With a GDP of over $900 billion, the Netherlands is one of the largest economies in Europe and a key player in the global economy.

One of the driving forces behind the Dutch economy is its robust trade and export sector. The Netherlands is strategically located at the crossroads of Europe, with excellent access to major markets in Western Europe, making it an ideal hub for international trade. Dutch companies are world leaders in sectors such as agriculture, chemicals, machinery, electronics, and pharmaceuticals, exporting goods and services to countries around the world.

The Port of Rotterdam is a crucial linchpin of the Dutch economy, serving as one of the busiest and most important seaports in the world. With state-of-the-art facilities, extensive transportation links, and a strategic location on the Rhine-Meuse-Scheldt delta, Rotterdam handles millions of tons of cargo each year, facilitating trade and commerce on a global scale. In addition to its thriving export sector, the Netherlands is also home to a dynamic and innovative technology industry. Dutch companies are at the forefront of innovation in fields such as high-tech manufacturing, renewable energy, biotechnology, and information technology. Startups and scale-ups in cities like Amsterdam, Eindhoven, and Utrecht are driving innovation and entrepreneurship, attracting investment and talent from around the world. The Dutch agricultural sector is another cornerstone of the economy, known for its efficiency, productivity, and sustainability. The Netherlands is one of the world's leading exporters of agricultural products, including fruits, vegetables, flowers, and dairy products. Dutch farmers are known for their innovative farming techniques, such as greenhouse cultivation and precision agriculture, which maximize yields while minimizing environmental impact.

Furthermore, the Netherlands has a strong financial services industry, with Amsterdam serving as one of Europe's leading financial centers. Dutch banks, insurance companies, and asset management firms play a vital role in facilitating international trade, providing financing and risk management services to businesses and investors worldwide.

The Dutch government plays an active role in supporting economic growth and development through policies aimed at promoting innovation, entrepreneurship, and sustainability. Initiatives such as InvestNL and StartupDelta provide support and resources to startups and scale-ups, helping them to grow and succeed in the global marketplace.

Overall, the Dutch economy is characterized by its resilience, diversity, and innovation, with a strong foundation built on trade, technology, agriculture, and finance. Despite challenges such as global economic uncertainty and environmental concerns, the Netherlands continues to thrive and prosper, demonstrating its ability to adapt and succeed in a rapidly changing world.

Dutch Environmental Initiatives: Sustainability in Action

Dutch environmental initiatives are at the forefront of global efforts to combat climate change and promote sustainability. As a low-lying country with a vulnerable coastline and a history of water management challenges, the Netherlands has long recognized the importance of environmental stewardship and sustainable development.

One of the key pillars of Dutch environmental initiatives is renewable energy. The Netherlands is committed to transitioning to a low-carbon economy by increasing the use of renewable energy sources such as wind, solar, and biomass. Offshore wind farms in the North Sea generate a significant portion of the country's electricity, with ambitious plans to expand offshore wind capacity in the coming years. Solar panels are also becoming increasingly common on rooftops and in fields across the country, harnessing the power of the sun to generate clean, renewable energy. In addition to renewable energy, the Netherlands is actively working to reduce its carbon footprint and promote energy efficiency. The Dutch government has implemented a range of policies and incentives to encourage energy conservation and sustainable practices, such as subsidies for energy-efficient home improvements, tax breaks for electric vehicles, and energy efficiency standards for buildings and appliances.

Water management is another area where Dutch environmental initiatives excel. The Netherlands is a global leader in flood control, coastal protection, and water quality management, with a comprehensive system of dikes, dams, and flood barriers designed to protect against flooding and sea-level rise. The Delta Works, a series of massive engineering projects built in response to devastating floods in the 20th century, is a testament to Dutch ingenuity and innovation in water management. Furthermore, the Netherlands is committed to promoting sustainable transportation and reducing greenhouse gas emissions from the transportation sector. Dutch cities are known for their bike-friendly infrastructure, with extensive networks of bike lanes, paths, and bike-sharing programs that encourage cycling as a clean, efficient, and healthy mode of transportation. Public transportation is also highly efficient and accessible, with trains, buses, trams, and ferries providing convenient alternatives to driving.

The Dutch government has set ambitious targets for reducing carbon emissions and achieving carbon neutrality by 2050. Initiatives such as the Climate Agreement and the Green Deal aim to accelerate the transition to a sustainable economy by investing in renewable energy, promoting energy efficiency, and reducing emissions from industry, agriculture, and transportation.

In summary, Dutch environmental initiatives are comprehensive, ambitious, and forward-thinking, reflecting the country's commitment to sustainability and environmental stewardship. By embracing renewable energy, promoting energy efficiency, and investing in innovative solutions to environmental challenges, the Netherlands is leading by example and demonstrating that a sustainable future is within reach.

Dutch Social Welfare: Ensuring Equality

Dutch social welfare programs are designed to ensure equality and provide support to all members of society, regardless of their socioeconomic status. The Netherlands has a comprehensive system of social security that includes benefits and services aimed at meeting the basic needs of its citizens and residents.

One of the cornerstones of Dutch social welfare is the healthcare system. The Netherlands has a universal healthcare system based on mandatory health insurance, ensuring that everyone has access to essential medical care. Basic health insurance covers a wide range of services, including doctor visits, hospital care, prescription medications, and mental health treatment. Low-income individuals and families may be eligible for additional subsidies to help cover the cost of health insurance premiums.

In addition to healthcare, the Dutch government provides a variety of social benefits to support individuals and families in need. These benefits include unemployment benefits, disability benefits, housing assistance, and child support. The goal of these programs is to ensure that everyone has access to a decent standard of living and can participate fully in society, regardless of their circumstances.

The Netherlands also has a strong focus on education and childcare as part of its social welfare system. Public education is free and compulsory for children between the ages of 5 and 16, ensuring that all children have access to quality education regardless of their family's income. Additionally, the Dutch government provides subsidies for childcare to help working parents cover the cost of childcare services, making it easier for families to balance work and family life.

Furthermore, the Netherlands has a progressive tax system that redistributes wealth and supports social welfare programs. High-income individuals and corporations pay higher tax rates, which help fund social security benefits and public services. This system of progressive taxation helps ensure that the burden of financing social welfare programs is shared fairly across society.

The Dutch government also invests in initiatives to promote social inclusion and integration, particularly for immigrants and refugees. Programs such as language courses, job training, and cultural integration classes help newcomers adjust to life in the Netherlands and become active participants in their communities.

Overall, Dutch social welfare programs play a crucial role in promoting equality, reducing poverty, and fostering social cohesion. By providing access to healthcare, education, social benefits, and support services, the Netherlands ensures that everyone has the opportunity to live a dignified and fulfilling life, regardless of their background or circumstances.

Dutch Immigration: Diversity and Integration

Dutch immigration has played a significant role in shaping the cultural, social, and economic landscape of the Netherlands. Over the years, the country has welcomed immigrants from various parts of the world, contributing to its diversity and richness.

Historically, immigration to the Netherlands has been influenced by factors such as colonialism, labor migration, and refugee flows. In the post-World War II era, the Netherlands experienced waves of immigration from former Dutch colonies in Indonesia, Suriname, and the Dutch Antilles, leading to the establishment of vibrant diaspora communities in the Netherlands.

In addition to colonial migration, labor migration has been a key driver of immigration to the Netherlands. In the 1960s and 1970s, the Dutch government recruited guest workers from countries such as Turkey, Morocco, and Spain to address labor shortages in sectors such as manufacturing and construction. Many of these guest workers eventually settled in the Netherlands, bringing their families and contributing to the country's cultural and ethnic diversity. In more recent years, the Netherlands has also welcomed refugees and asylum seekers fleeing conflict, persecution, and humanitarian crises in countries such as Syria, Afghanistan, and Iraq. The Dutch government has a long-standing tradition of providing refuge to those in need, offering shelter, protection, and support to individuals and families seeking safety and security. Integration is a key focus of Dutch immigration policy, with efforts aimed at facilitating the social, cultural, and economic integration of immigrants into Dutch society. Integration programs and initiatives provide newcomers with language courses, civic education, job training, and support services to help them adjust to life in the Netherlands and become active participants in their communities.

Despite efforts to promote integration, challenges remain, particularly in areas such as employment, education, and social cohesion. Immigrants and their descendants often face barriers to accessing employment opportunities and achieving socioeconomic mobility, leading to disparities in outcomes between immigrant and native-born populations.

Furthermore, issues such as discrimination, cultural differences, and social exclusion can pose challenges to integration efforts, creating tensions and divisions within society. However, the Netherlands continues to work towards fostering inclusivity, diversity, and social cohesion through policies and initiatives aimed at promoting understanding, tolerance, and mutual respect among all members of society.

Overall, Dutch immigration has contributed to the cultural, social, and economic vitality of the Netherlands, enriching the country's identity and fostering a sense of global interconnectedness. By embracing diversity and promoting integration, the Netherlands strives to build a more inclusive and cohesive society where everyone has the opportunity to thrive and contribute to the common good.

Dutch Influence on Global Culture

The influence of Dutch culture on the global stage is profound and far-reaching, spanning centuries and leaving an indelible mark on various aspects of art, commerce, science, and beyond. One of the most notable contributions of Dutch culture to the global stage is its rich artistic heritage. During the Dutch Golden Age in the 17th century, artists such as Rembrandt van Rijn, Johannes Vermeer, and Vincent van Gogh produced masterpieces that continue to captivate audiences around the world. Dutch painters pioneered techniques such as chiaroscuro and genre painting, influencing subsequent generations of artists and shaping the course of Western art history.

Beyond the realm of fine art, Dutch influence extends to literature and philosophy. Dutch authors and thinkers have made significant contributions to world literature and intellectual discourse. Philosophers such as Desiderius Erasmus, known for his humanist writings, and Baruch Spinoza, renowned for his rationalist philosophy, have left a lasting legacy on the global intellectual landscape. Dutch literature, ranging from classic works like "The Diary of Anne Frank" to contemporary novels by authors such as Herman Koch and Arnon Grunberg, continues to resonate with readers worldwide, offering insights into Dutch culture and society.

In the realm of commerce, the Dutch have played a pivotal role in shaping global trade and finance. The

Dutch East India Company, founded in the 17th century, was one of the world's first multinational corporations, dominating trade routes between Europe, Asia, and Africa and laying the groundwork for modern capitalism. The Amsterdam Stock Exchange, established in 1602, is one of the oldest stock exchanges in the world and continues to be a leading center for international finance.

Dutch innovation and engineering prowess have also left their mark on the global stage. The Dutch are known for their expertise in water management and hydraulic engineering, developing innovative solutions to mitigate the risks of flooding and protect against sea-level rise. Projects such as the Delta Works, a series of massive flood defense systems, and the Afsluitdijk, a monumental dike that spans the width of the IJsselmeer, showcase Dutch ingenuity and engineering excellence.

Furthermore, Dutch culture has influenced global trends in design, architecture, and urban planning. Dutch architects and designers are renowned for their minimalist aesthetics, functional approach, and sustainable design principles. Icons of Dutch design, such as the works of Gerrit Rietveld and the Bauhaus-influenced De Stijl movement, have inspired generations of designers and architects worldwide.

In the realm of technology and innovation, the Netherlands continues to be a leader, particularly in sectors such as renewable energy, agriculture, and logistics. Dutch companies and research institutions are at the forefront of developing sustainable technologies and solutions to address pressing global challenges, such as climate change and food security.

Overall, Dutch influence on global culture is multifaceted and enduring, spanning art, literature, commerce, innovation, and more. Through its rich cultural heritage, spirit of entrepreneurship, and commitment to innovation and sustainability, the Netherlands continues to make a significant impact on the world stage, shaping the course of history and leaving a legacy that resonates across continents and generations.

Dutch Language and Dialects

The Dutch language, known as Nederlands, is the official language of the Netherlands, Belgium, Suriname, and parts of the Caribbean. It belongs to the West Germanic branch of the Indo-European language family and is closely related to German and English. Dutch is spoken by over 23 million people worldwide, making it one of the major languages of Europe.

Standard Dutch, also known as Algemeen Beschaafd Nederlands (ABN), serves as the standard form of the language used in formal settings, education, media, and government. It is based on the dialect spoken in the Randstad region, which includes cities like Amsterdam, Rotterdam, The Hague, and Utrecht. Standard Dutch is characterized by its relatively neutral pronunciation and grammatical structure, making it easily understood by speakers from different regions.

Despite the prevalence of Standard Dutch, the Netherlands is home to a rich diversity of regional dialects and accents. These dialects vary significantly in pronunciation, vocabulary, and grammar, reflecting the country's regional and cultural diversity. In the northern province of Friesland, for example, Frisian is spoken alongside Dutch, and it holds official status in the region.

In addition to regional dialects, Dutch has also been influenced by other languages, particularly through historical contact and trade. The Dutch colonial empire once spanned across Asia, Africa, and the Americas, resulting in the adoption of loanwords from languages such as Malay, Indonesian, Javanese, and Sranan Tongo. Furthermore, the proximity of the Netherlands to other European countries has led to the incorporation of loanwords from French, English, German, and Spanish into the Dutch vocabulary.

Dutch is known for its relatively straightforward grammatical structure, with a subject-verb-object word order and a system of two genders (common and neuter). Nouns are inflected for number (singular or plural), while verbs conjugate based on tense, mood, and aspect. Dutch pronunciation can vary depending on the region, with differences in vowel sounds, consonant pronunciation, and intonation patterns.

In recent years, Dutch has also seen the emergence of youth slang, influenced by popular culture, social media, and multiculturalism. These new linguistic developments reflect the dynamic nature of language and its ability to evolve over time in response to changing social and cultural contexts.

Overall, Dutch language and dialects are integral parts of the cultural identity of the Netherlands, reflecting the country's rich linguistic heritage and diversity. From Standard Dutch to regional dialects and contemporary slang, the Dutch language continues to evolve and adapt, shaping communication and identity in the modern world.

Dutch Etiquette and Social Customs

Navigating Dutch etiquette and social customs can be a fascinating journey into the heart of Dutch culture, which values directness, egalitarianism, and respect for personal space. One of the key aspects of Dutch etiquette is the concept of "gezelligheid," which roughly translates to coziness, conviviality, and a sense of togetherness. Whether it's sharing a meal with friends or gathering for a gezellig evening at home, creating a warm and inviting atmosphere is highly prized in Dutch social interactions.

When greeting someone in the Netherlands, a firm handshake and direct eye contact are customary, along with a simple "hallo" or "goedemorgen" (good morning) depending on the time of day. It's common for Dutch people to address each other by their first names, regardless of age or social status, reflecting the country's egalitarian ethos.

In social settings, punctuality is appreciated, and it's considered polite to arrive on time for appointments, meetings, and social gatherings. However, the Dutch also value efficiency and pragmatism, so it's acceptable to be direct and to the point in conversations, without excessive small talk or pleasantries.

Dutch dining etiquette is relatively informal compared to some other cultures. When invited to someone's home for a meal, it's customary to bring a small gift, such as flowers or wine, as a token of appreciation. Seating arrangements are often informal, with guests typically seated around the table in a casual manner. It's polite to wait for the host or hostess to begin eating before starting your meal, and it's customary to use utensils rather than eating with your hands.

In terms of social hierarchy, the Dutch tend to be egalitarian and value equality. This is reflected in their communication style, which is direct and straightforward. It's common for Dutch people to express their opinions openly and honestly, even if it means disagreeing with others. However, this directness should not be mistaken for rudeness; rather, it's a reflection of the Dutch preference for clear and transparent communication.

When it comes to socializing, the Dutch enjoy spending time outdoors and participating in recreational activities such as cycling, hiking, and boating. These activities provide opportunities for relaxation and socializing in a relaxed and informal setting. Additionally, the Netherlands has a vibrant cafe culture, with outdoor terraces bustling with activity, especially during the warmer months.

Overall, understanding Dutch etiquette and social customs can help visitors and newcomers navigate social interactions with ease and confidence. By embracing the values of gezelligheid, egalitarianism, and direct communication, you can experience the warmth and hospitality of Dutch culture firsthand.

Exploring Dutch Countryside: Villages and Landscapes

Exploring the Dutch countryside unveils a picturesque landscape dotted with charming villages, verdant fields, and winding waterways. Beyond the bustling cities, the Netherlands boasts a tranquil countryside that beckons visitors to discover its hidden treasures and idyllic landscapes.

One of the defining features of the Dutch countryside is its extensive network of canals and waterways, which crisscross the land like veins, shaping the landscape and providing a lifeline for transportation and agriculture. Canal-side villages such as Giethoorn and Kinderdijk offer a glimpse into traditional Dutch life, with historic houses, quaint bridges, and serene waterways evoking a sense of timeless beauty.

The Dutch countryside is also characterized by its picturesque windmills, iconic symbols of the Netherlands' centuries-old battle against water. These towering structures, once used to pump water out of low-lying areas and grind grain, now stand as enduring monuments to Dutch engineering prowess and ingenuity. The Kinderdijk windmills, a UNESCO World Heritage site, are among the most famous examples, offering visitors a glimpse into the country's rich maritime history.

Beyond windmills and canals, the Dutch countryside is a patchwork of lush green fields, colorful flower fields, and meandering rivers. In the spring, the countryside bursts into bloom with vibrant tulip fields stretching as far as the eye can see, creating a kaleidoscope of colors that captivates visitors from around the world. The Keukenhof Gardens, located near Lisse, are a popular destination for experiencing the beauty of Dutch tulips in full bloom.

Throughout the countryside, picturesque villages offer a glimpse into traditional Dutch life, with charming cobblestone streets, historic churches, and cozy cafes. Each village has its own unique character and charm, whether it's the cheese markets of Edam and Gouda or the quaint fishing villages of Volendam and Marken.

For outdoor enthusiasts, the Dutch countryside offers a wealth of opportunities for exploration and adventure. Cycling is a popular pastime in the Netherlands, and the countryside is crisscrossed with scenic bike paths that wind through meadows, forests, and along the coast. Hiking trails offer opportunities to explore the country's diverse landscapes, from coastal dunes to heathlands and woodlands teeming with wildlife.

In conclusion, exploring the Dutch countryside is a journey of discovery, offering visitors a chance to immerse themselves in the natural beauty, rich history, and timeless charm of rural Netherlands. Whether wandering through quaint villages, cycling along scenic pathways, or admiring windmills against a backdrop of tulip fields, the Dutch countryside never fails to captivate and inspire.

Planning Your Visit: Essential Travel Tips for the Netherlands

Planning a visit to the Netherlands opens the door to a world of vibrant culture, stunning landscapes, and rich history. To make the most of your trip, it's essential to prepare wisely and familiarize yourself with some essential travel tips tailored to the Dutch experience.

First and foremost, consider the best time to visit. The Netherlands enjoys a temperate maritime climate, characterized by mild summers and relatively mild winters. However, the weather can be unpredictable, so it's wise to pack layers and be prepared for rain at any time of year. Spring (March to May) is particularly popular, as it brings the famous Dutch tulip season into full bloom, painting the countryside with vibrant colors.

When it comes to transportation, the Netherlands boasts an efficient and extensive public transportation network, including trains, trams, buses, and ferries. The Dutch railway system, operated by Nederlandse Spoorwegen (NS), connects major cities and towns, making it easy to travel between destinations. Consider purchasing an OV-chipkaart, a rechargeable smart card that allows for seamless travel on public transport throughout the country.

While public transportation is convenient, cycling is also a popular and practical way to explore the

Netherlands, thanks to its flat terrain and extensive network of bike paths. Renting a bicycle is easy and affordable, and it provides a unique opportunity to experience the country like a local. Just remember to follow traffic rules and respect cyclists' right of way.

When it comes to accommodation, the Netherlands offers a wide range of options to suit every budget and preference. From boutique hotels and charming bed and breakfasts to hostels and campgrounds, there's something for everyone. Booking accommodations in advance, especially during peak tourist seasons, is advisable to ensure availability and secure the best rates.

As for dining, the Netherlands is a culinary paradise with a diverse array of delicious dishes to savor. Don't miss out on trying traditional Dutch specialties such as stroopwafels, bitterballen, and stamppot. Additionally, the Netherlands is known for its cheese, so be sure to sample some authentic Gouda or Edam cheese during your visit.

Finally, be sure to explore beyond the tourist hotspots and immerse yourself in Dutch culture and daily life. Take time to wander through charming neighborhoods, visit local markets, and interact with friendly locals. Whether you're exploring the bustling streets of Amsterdam, cycling through picturesque countryside, or admiring historic windmills, the Netherlands offers a wealth of unforgettable experiences for travelers of all interests.

Epilogue

As we come to the end of our journey through the vibrant tapestry of Dutch culture, history, and landscape, it's worth reflecting on the rich experiences and insights gained along the way.

Throughout this exploration, we've delved into the Netherlands' fascinating history, from its Golden Age of trade and innovation to its struggles during World War II and its emergence as a modern progressive society. We've marveled at the iconic windmills and tulip fields, wandered through picturesque villages, and savored the flavors of Dutch cuisine.

We've learned about the Dutch commitment to environmental sustainability, their pioneering spirit in technology and engineering, and their emphasis on social welfare and inclusivity. We've celebrated the country's cultural heritage, from its world-renowned art and architecture to its vibrant music and literature scene.

But perhaps most importantly, we've gained a deeper appreciation for the Dutch spirit of tolerance, openness, and acceptance. In a world often divided by differences, the Netherlands serves as a shining example of a society that values diversity, equality, and mutual respect.

As we bid farewell to this captivating land of tulips and windmills, may we carry with us the lessons learned and the memories cherished. Whether it's the warmth of a gezellig evening with friends, the beauty of a Dutch landscape bathed in golden light, or the inspiring stories of resilience and innovation, the Netherlands leaves an indelible mark on all who visit.

So, as we turn the final page of this journey, let us remember the words of the Dutch proverb: "Doe maar gewoon, dan doe je al gek genoeg" – "Just act normal, that's crazy enough." In a world of complexity and uncertainty, let us strive to embrace simplicity, authenticity, and the timeless values that define the Dutch spirit. And who knows, perhaps one day we'll find ourselves returning to this enchanting land, ready to embark on a new adventure and create more unforgettable memories.

Printed in Great Britain
by Amazon